The Importance of Inspiration

The Importance
of Inspiration

by

James T. Jeremiah, M.A., D.D.

REGULAR BAPTIST PRESS
1800 Oakton Boulevard
Des Plaines, Illinois 60018

Library of Congress catalogue card number: 76-187282

Printed in the United States of America

To my wife, Ruby, whose love and encouragement have been of inestimable help throughout my ministry.

CONTENTS

FOREWORD

Can we know for sure whether the Bible comes from God or not? The origin and authority of the Bible is the crucial question for every individual to settle. If the Bible is the book of God, as it most certainly claims to be, it is of the utmost importance to acknowledge this fact, to admit its claims and to acclaim its message to a needy world. James T. Jeremiah writes with the firm conviction that no other fact in the universe is founded on so much and such convincing evidence as the inspiration of the Bible.

Dr. Jeremiah masterfully marshals his material and presents it in readable, refreshing style. As a pastor for many years and as President of Cedarville College for the past eighteen years, Dr. Jeremiah has faithfully proclaimed the Bible as the inerrant, infallible Word of God. His preaching and teaching have always strengthened the faith of his listeners. I am sure this book will likewise deepen the faith of its readers.

In a day of neo-evangelical timidity and neo-orthodox trifling with reference to the inspiration of the Bible, Dr. Jeremiah trumpets a clear, certain testimony concerning the verbal-plenary inspiration of the Word of God. While all of the book was of distinct blessing to me, the chapter entitled "The Importance of Inspiration to the Expository Preacher" was especially helpful. It is indeed a signal honor for me to recommend this book to pastors, teachers and Bible students everywhere.

Paul Tassell, Ph.D.
NATIONAL YOUTH REPRESENTATIVE
OF THE GENERAL ASSOCIATION OF
REGULAR BAPTIST CHURCHES

INTRODUCTION

Church history reveals that every age has its own doctrinal problems. The verbal, plenary inspiration of the Scriptures has been thrown into the theological arena of our generation. Many years ago Dr. James Orr predicted that this would be true.

> That battle will have to be fought, if I mistake not, in the first instance, around the fortress of the work and authority of Holy Scripture. A doctrine of Scripture adapted to the needs of the hour, harmonizing with the demands at once of science and of faith is perhaps the most claimant want at present in theology; but the whole conception of Christianity will get drawn in and many of the old controversies will be revived in new forms.[1]

In this battle we have the fundamentalist on one hand who insists on a trustworthy Bible; and on the other, the liberal and the neo-orthodox, both promoters of the ecumenical movement who consider an inspired Bible not only to be of little importance, but rather a hindrance to a falsely-founded church union. In order to unite Christendom in one great religious force, the inspiration of the Bible and resultant doctrines are by these men considered to be of little consequence: sincerity of attitude is a substitute for sound doctrine in order to make one church. This will lead to an ever-increasing dependence on centralized ecclesiastical authority and develop into a philosophy similar to that of the Jewish Sanhedrin where tradition and human reason, rather than the Word of God, become the basis for one's faith.

---

[1] James Orr, *The Progress of Dogma* (New York: George H. Doran Company, 1901), p. 352.

The doctrine of inspiration is of vital importance since there can be no Biblical infallibility and authority without it.

> If the Bible is not infallible, then we can be sure of nothing. The other doctrines of Christianity will then, one by one, go by the board. The fortunes of Christianity stand or fall with an infallible Bible. Attempts to evade this conclusion can only lead to self-deception.[2]

It does matter very much whether or not we have an inspired Bible. There can be no Christianity without it.

This brings us to the next question of importance regarding this theme. Inspiration, yes, but which of the many views on the subject is the correct one? The majority in Christendom will say that the Bible is inspired after a fashion; so if we insist that inspiration is important, we must define our terms.

The Dictation Theory. This view presents the writers of the Bible as passive instruments of the Holy Spirit. This they were not, since the Bible is not written with a uniform style. For example, Paul had a special interest not expressed by others (Rom. 9:1-3). Above the cross was a superscription variously reported by the Gospel writers (John 19:19; Luke 23:38) which would have been the same exact wording in each Gospel had the record been a dictation. God would have dictated the same words in each instance. Strong says this theory is "inconsistent with a wise economy of means to suppose that the Scripture writers should have had dictated to them what they knew already or what they could inform themselves of by the use of their natural powers."[3]

The Intuition Theory. All Christians are said to have spiritual equipment for special service, and in this way the writers of the Bible were enabled to write. This view

---

[2] Edward J. Young, *Thy Word is Truth* (Grand Rapids: William B. Eerdmans Publishing House, 1957), p. 5.

[3] Augustus Hopkins Strong, *Systematic Theology* (Philadelphia: Griffith and Rowland Press, 1907), p. 210.

gives foundation for the many new and contradictory cults which claim extrabiblical revelation. This result is to be expected since what one man claims to be inspired, another man is inspired to pronounce as ideas. The Bible does not teach this inspiration by intuition. Paul was not inspired to write his epistles and another man inspired to reject them. This theory makes man the highest and final authority since this inspiration comes from him. One who claims such inspiration denies a personal God Who is Truth and the Revealer of truth. Certainly 2 Timothy 3:16 and 2 Peter 1:21 teach us that Biblical inspiration is more than the infilling of the Spirit for service.

The Partial Theory. According to this position, inspiration has reference only to truths unknown or unknowable to human research. It does not claim inspiration for the literary, historical or scientific elements in Scripture. In refutation of this view, we say that though it is not a textbook in these areas, the Bible does speak truthfully about them wherever they are mentioned in the history of redemption which is one of the great themes of the Bible. Christ accepted *all* of the Old Testament as authentic. "And beginning at Moses and *all* the prophets, he expounded unto them in *all* the scriptures the things concerning himself" (Luke 24:27, *italics ours*).

The Conceptual Theory. The thoughts, not the words of Scripture, are inspired is the idea presented in this view. The ideas were imparted to the human authors who clothed these thoughts in their own words. The Bible itself repudiates this in 1 Corinthians 2:13, "Which things also we speak, not in the words which man's wisdom teacheth, but which the Holy Ghost teacheth; comparing spiritual things with spiritual." Since a word is a vehicle by which thought is communicated from one person to another, it is difficult to understand how one can think without the use of words.

The Natural Theory. One who holds to natural inspiration says that the Bible is a masterpiece similar to the productions of exceptional musicians, poets and artists. It is the product of human genius rather than divine inspiration. The Bible claims a higher source for its origin, for "All scripture is given by inspiration of God. . ." (2 Tim. 3:16).

The Neo-Orthodox Theory. The natural theory of inspiration which substituted an inspired experience for an inspired text was soon followed by the neo-orthodox attack which teaches that "The Scriptures are at best a fallible witness to revelation."[4] To one who holds the neo-orthodox position, the Bible becomes the Word of God when it speaks to, or overpowers us. When the Bible creates faith in us, it is then to us the inspired Word of God. The Bible is the Word of God so far as God allows it to be such and speaks through it. This means that the Bible could be, and to the Barthian is, a book produced by man and filled with errors. To men who hold this view, some parts of the Bible are more authoritative than others because they tend to speak more of Christ. Ryrie sums up the view when he writes, "Their doctrine includes orthodox terminology built on liberal exegesis. It attempts to have inspiration without infallibility; authority without actuality."[5]

The Biblical View of Inspiration. What does the Bible actually teach regarding its own inspiration? "All scripture is given by inspiration of God, and is profitable for doctrine, for reproof, for correction, for instruction in righteousness: That the man of God may be perfect, throughly furnished unto all good works" (2 Tim. 3:16). The meaning of this verse has been summarized by Dr. Merrill F. Unger in the following words:

---

[4] Charles C. Ryrie, "The Importance of Inerrancy," *Bibliotheca Sacra,* CXX, April-June, 1963 (Dallas: Dallas Theological Seminary), p. 139.

[5] Charles C. Ryrie, *Neo-Orthodoxy, What It Is, and What It Does* (Chicago: Moody Press, 1956), p. 48.

This pivotal passage in the plainest possible terms teaches five great truths: first, the plenary inspiration of the Bible — "all"; secondly, the plenary inspiration specifically of the Old Testament — (later, when the sacred canon was completed, the New Testament, also) "all Scripture"; thirdly, the divine authorship of the Scripture — "given by inspiration of God"; fourthly, the supreme value of all Scripture to the spiritual life because of its inspiration and consequent authority — "profitable for doctrine, for reproof, for correction, for instruction in righteousness"; fifthly, the holy purpose of Scripture — "that the man of God may be perfect (or complete), throughly furnished unto all good works."[6]

All scripture is inspired; that is, God-breathed. We believe the words were chosen of God so that the writers recorded precisely what God wanted revealed. "Our basic affirmation is that in employing language, God saw to it that the right words were used in the right way at the right time."[7]

This passage in 2 Timothy is not the only and isolated text which suggests the verbal, plenary inspiration of the Scripture. In prophetic language the Lord spoke to Moses, saying, "I will raise them up a Prophet from among their brethren, like unto thee, and will put my words in his mouth; and he shall speak unto them all that I shall command him" (Deut. 18:18). To Jeremiah the prophet God said, "Behold, I have put my words in thy mouth. . . and arise, and speak unto them all that I command thee. . ." (Jer. 1:9, 17). In the New Testament Christ promised the writers of the New Testament infallible communication by the Holy Spirit (John 14:26). The early Christians accepted this message "not as the word of men, but as it is in truth, the

[6] Merrill F. Unger, "The Inspiration of the Old Testament," *Bibliotheca Sacra*, CVII, October-December, 1950, (Dallas: Dallas Theological Seminary), pp. 432, 433.

[7] William Fitch, *The Impregnable Rock of Holy Scripture* (Toronto: Toronto Bible College, 1965), p. 7.

word of God. . ." (1 Thess. 2:13). Peter testified to the inspiration of the Scriptures when he wrote, "Holy men of God spake as they were moved by the Holy Ghost" (2 Peter 1:21).

The phrase, "Thus saith the Lord", or its equivalent, occurs about two thousand times in the Old Testament. If these Biblical quotations mean anything, they do teach that "Those to whom God gave His revelation were men born of the Holy Spirit, whose messages were infallibly delivered and absolutely free from error, being precisely the words that God Himself wished to have declared."[8]

---

[8] Young, *op. cit.*, p. 45.

I

THE IMPORTANCE OF
INSPIRATION TO BIBLICAL
AUTHORITY

Prior to the Dark Ages and following the Reformation, Christians accepted the Bible as authoritative. The Church Fathers assumed the inspiration of the Scriptures as a self-evident truth. Inspiration and infallibility were emphasized by the reformers in opposition to the Roman Catholic theology which declares the church to be infallible.

Bible-believing Christians in the early post-apostolic and Reformation periods affirmed that "The Holy Scriptures are the ultimate authority, the Supreme Court, so to speak, whose decisions are final in all matters pertaining to Christian faith and practice."[9] Romanism, on the other hand, has made the church itself the final authority. The Bible, to many in our time, is an authority only as it may agree with the intellectual conclusions of modern man. We have, therefore, three "authorities" clamoring for recognition: revelation, Romanism and rationalism.

---

[9] George P. Pardington, *Outline Studies in Christian Doctrine* (Harrisburg: Christian Publications, 1926), p. 52.

That the authority of the Bible is dependent upon full and verbal inspiration seems obvious.

> The concept of the Bible as a special revelation grows out of the doctrine of the authority of God's Word. The authority of the Bible rests upon the infallibility of the Scriptures. In turn, the basis of the infallibility of Scripture is its verbal, plenary inspiration.[10]

If God has not given His Word to men through His chosen vessels, then the Bible is of no more authority than any human document, and consequently of less authority than a church which claims to be founded upon Christ or human reason which asserts itself as the ultimate answer to every question. The Biblical view of inspiration assures us of the following salient facts.

A. AN AUTHORITY WHICH IS CREDIBLE

In the discussion of this topic, the definition of terms is important. By the credibility of the Scriptures, we mean that they are inerrant and infallable. By inerrancy we mean the Bible is wholly true, and by infallibility we mean that the Bible is incapable of error or wholly trustworthy. Though there is a slight difference in the meaning of these two words, as far as our present approach is concerned we wish to emphasize our conviction that the Bible can be depended upon. To the Christian, therefore, the Bible is, and should be, fully authoritative.

Although this position of an authoritative Bible based upon plenary inspiration would seem to be an obvious conclusion to all professing Christians, such is not the case in the present hour. There are attempts in our day to separate verbal inspiration from inerrancy. One writer states it thus:

---

[10] John A. Witmer, "The Twentieth Century—Battleground of Bibliography" *Bibliotheca Sacra*, CXI, October-December, 1954, (Dallas: Dallas Theological Seminary), p. 106.

Unquestionably, the Bible teaches its own inspiration. It is the Book of God. It does not require us to hold inerrancy, though this is a natural corollary of full inspiration. The phenomena which present difficulties are not to be dismissed or underrated. They have driven many sincere believers in the trustworthiness of the Bible as a spiritual guide to hold a modified position on the non-revelation material. Every man must be persuaded in his own mind . . . . It is possible that if our own knowledge were greater, all seeming difficulties could be swept away.[11]

To the contrary, Dr. Edward J. Young states,

There is no such thing as inspiration which does not carry with it the correlate of infallibility. A Bible that is fallible—and we speak, of course, of the original—is a Bible which is not inspired. A Bible that is inspired is a Bible that is infallible. There is no middle ground.[12]

Inspiration is important to infallibility because the God Who inspired the Word is Himself infallible, and therefore He could not do less than provide an infallible record for His people. "God is true" (John 3:33) is a fact supported by these statements: "That they might know thee, the only true God" (John 17:3) ; "Let God be true, but every man a liar" (Rom. 3:4) ; "Serve the living and true God" (I Thess. 1:9) ; "God, that cannot lie, promised" (Titus 1:2). It is impossible to fully believe that the God of truth can inspire the Bible, and at the same time hold that it is full of error.

What Scripture says is to be received as the infallible word of the infallible God; and to assert biblical inerrancy and infallibility is just to confess faith in (1) the divine origin of the Bible, and (2) the truthfulness and trustworthiness of God.[13]

---

[11] Everett F. Harrison, "The Phenomena of Scripture," in *The Revelation and the Bible,* edited by Carl F. H. Henry (Grand Rapids: Baker Book House, 1958), p. 250.

[12] Young, *op. cit.,* pp. 108, 109.

[13] J. I. Packer, *Fundamentalism and the Word of God* (Grand Rapids: William B. Eerdmans Publishing House, 1958), pp. 95, 96.

Men reject the infallibility of the Scriptures because they are not willing to believe in the infallibility of God nor accept what the Bible teaches concerning its own inspiration.

If the Bible is not an inerrant authority, such statements as made by Jesus in Matthew 5:18 have no meaning: "For verily I say unto you, Till heaven and earth pass, one jot or one tittle shall in no wise pass from the law, till all be fulfilled." The jot is the smallest stroke which distinguishes certain Hebrew letters from one another. This minute detail could not be guaranteed unless the God of truth inspired the record. When so inspired in detail, the Word of God proves to be infallible.

The Bible is an authority in doctrine because it states God's truth in these areas. Scriptures are authoritative whether or not God speaks through them to the individual. The majority of contemporary theologians who say that the Bible is inspired only when God speaks to the individual through them will also teach that the same God often gives an inspired message through writings of human origin. No wonder we have a confused theological picture in our day.

How can one know the truth, for example, about the doctrine of the Person and work of Christ if he does not accept what the Bible teaches about Him? Actually, the only certain knowledge we have about Christ we find in the Bible. In spite of this obvious fact, there are some who accept the position that one can believe in a kind of inspiration without believing in the authority of the Book so inspired. An outstanding Christian leader of our generation, in an article printed in the November, 1958 issue of *Eternity* magazine (pp. 18, 19) said, "I do not believe that the ground of our fellowship is to be the inerrancy of Scripture, but rather the ground of our fellowship is to be the deity of our Lord Jesus Christ." Will someone tell us how we have any authority to believe in the deity of Christ if the Bible record is not trustworthy? He continues, "I, myself, hold to the verbal inspiration viewpoint. . . . Yet I know devout men of God who believe in the virgin birth, the atonement, the resurrection, and who have strong evangelistic zeal and passion who do not hold to this particular theory of inspiration." How can one actually believe in the virgin birth, atonement, resurrection and the other great doctrines of the faith if he does not accept the verbal, plenary inspiration of the Biblical record? On what authority can we believe these doctrines if the Bible is not inerrant and infallible? The verbal, plenary inspiration of the Scriptures is the foundation of all other doctrines of our faith. We have no basis for believing the doctrines of Christianity if they are not based upon Biblical authority. Furthermore, we cannot comprehend their relationship one to the other if they are not inseparably related in a Bible true in all of its parts.

B. AN AUTHORITY WHICH IS DURABLE

Authority imposed upon men by the councils of other men will change in one way or another over the years. What one scholar writes today may be completely reversed in a year or so. It is conceivable that what a church organization teaches today, it may not teach tomorrow. Nowhere is this better illustrated than in the apostasy existent in many of the great denominations of our time. What the founders of these churches accepted as authority is no longer the basis of what these same denominations teach now. Revelation has been substituted by rationalism.

"Rome never changes." Perhaps within certain limitations this could have been said a few years ago, but not today. The ecumenical emphasis within the Roman Catholic Church has made this motto difficult to defend. Roman Catholic authority has changed. It has become more Protestant and at the same time Protestantism has become more Romish.

Jesus makes a higher claim for His words than is accepted by many religious leaders in the present hour.

He said, "Heaven and earth shall pass away, but my words shall not pass away" (Matt. 24:35). One would not expect the words of the eternal God to pass away or change for of His Word it is said, "Thou hast magnified thy word above all thy name" (Psa. 138:2). It is as impossible to alter or destroy the Word of God as it is to destroy God Himself. "God is not a man, that he should lie; neither the son of man, that he should repent: hath he said, and shall he not do it? or hath he spoken, and shall he not make it good?" (Num. 23:19). What God promises, He does not forget, eliminate, nor change. What He predicts, He performs. What He says in His Word by inspiration will be as true tomorrow as the day when He caused it to be penned. "The doctrine of the LORD is perfect. . ." (Psa. 19:7—*marginal reference*). To assure us of the unchangeable, durable quality of the Word of God, He said, "My covenant will I not break, nor alter the thing that is gone out of my lips" (Psa. 89:34).

With such promises of durability for the Word of God, it is to be expected that Satan, the great enemy of God, will overlook no opportunity to destroy the Word of God which means so much to, and is so necessary for, His people. No Book has been so opposed by its enemies as has the Bible. There are countless illustrations of this antagonism. They go back in history to the garden of Eden where Satan asked, "Hath God said?" (Gen. 3:1) until the present day "God is dead" approach. Jehoiakim (600 B. C.) had his method of destroying the Word of God (Jer. 36:21-32) when he used his penknife on its pages and cast the roll into the fire. God said to Jeremiah, "Take thee again another roll, and write in it all the former words that were in the first roll. . ." (v. 28). Fire did not change nor destroy God's Word. If every copy could be burned, its truth is still "settled in heaven" (Psa. 119:89).

In A. D. 303 the Roman Emperor Diocletian ordered the

empire to be searched for copies of the Scriptures. Many valuable copies were confiscated and burned. The Emperor then erected a pillar on which he inscribed "Nomine Christianorum Extincto" (The name of the Christian Church is extinguished). However, when less than twenty-five years had passed, in A. D. 325 Emperor Constantine established the Scriptures in the church as the supreme rule of faith and life. God's Word had not been completely obliterated.

Infidels, atheists, agnostics, and freethinkers of the eighteenth and nineteenth centuries attacked the Bible from the intellectual point of view. Bolingbroke, Hume, Strauss, Graf, Wellhausen, Voltaire and others who led the attack have all passed off the scene but still the Word of God lives on.

The French infidel, Voltaire, died in 1778. Before his death, he predicted that within one hundred years after his departure Christianity would be forced out of existence. However, the British and Foreign Bible Society was founded in 1804, twenty-six years after Voltaire's prophecy. "His printing press with which he printed his infidel literature has since been used to print copies of the Word of God, and the very house in which he lived has been stacked with Bibles by the Geneva Bible Society."[14] How well this incident illustrates a similar victory recorded in Acts 19:20, "So mightily grew the word of God and prevailed."

The Bible has undergone many revisions, translations, paraphrases and versions, but nothing has been changed which would alter any major doctrine taught in the Scripture. It is a durable, unchanging authority because it is inspired by the Holy Spirit. Had this not been God's message, so inspired and preserved by His power, it would not have been able to withstand such treatment by either its foes or its friends.

---

[14] Sydney Collett, *All About the Bible*, Twentieth Edition (New York: Fleming H. Revell Company, n. d.), p. 63.

The Bible has had to fight its way through the millenniums with all odds against it. There has never been a time when it has not met opposition of some kind, often most bitter and intense, and yet it has come through the hostility, storms and vicissitudes of its history unscathed, secure and supreme. It will not drown; it will not burn; it will not be torn asunder. A divine power protects and promotes this Book . . . Like the mythical hydra of old with nine heads, any of which when cut away was replaced by two others, the Bible has multiplied with every assault upon it.[15]

C. AN AUTHORITY WHICH IS UNITED

It has been observed by many Bible students that though the Bible is generally considered to be one Book, it is actually a library of sixty-six books. These books are written by forty penmen who lived in different periods of time and came from various backgrounds. The Bible was some 1,400 years in composition. Humanly speaking, what unity can be expected from such diversity? In a rather extended quotation, Dr. A. T. Pierson points out just how impossible a united theme would be if the Bible were composed of mere human authors without the operation of the Holy Spirit's inspiration.

Imagine another book compiled by as many authors, scattered over as many centuries. Herodotus in the fifth century before Christ, contributes an historic fragment on the origin of all things. A century later, Aristotle adds a book on moral philosophy. Two centuries pass and Cicero adds a work on law and government. Still another hundred years and Virgil furnishes a grand point on ethics. In the next century Plutarch supplies some biographical sketches; nearly two hundred years after, Origen adds "Essays on Religious Creeds and Conduct." A century and a half later Augustine writes a treatise on theology, and Chrysostom a book of sermons.

---

[15] Gwynn McLendon Day, *The Wonders of the Word* (New York: Fleming H. Revell Company, 1907), p. 17.

Then seven centuries pass away and Abelard completes a compilation by a significant series on "Rhetoric and Scholastic Philosophy." And between these extremes which like the Bible spent fifteen centuries all along from Herodotus to Abelard, are thirty other countributors whose works enter into the final result—men from different nations, periods, habits, languages and education. Under the best conditions, how much real unity could be expected even if each successive contributor has read all that preceded his own fragment? In here, all are entirely at agreement: there is diversity in unity, and unity in diversity. It is e pluribus unum.[16]

From itself and for itself the Bible claims, "All Scripture is given by inspiration of God." "One cannot hold to inspiration and infallibility of certain parts and only the inspiration of other parts."[17] This means that the historical books of the Bible are as much inspired by the Spirit of God as are the poetical books of the Old Testament or the doctrinal books of the New Testament. God may have, and probably did use various means to communicate His will to the penmen of Scripture; but the recording of this revelation was so controlled by the Holy Spirit that the words were His own choosing.

In recent years the critics of the Bible have cast doubts upon the truthfulness of the historical books. Yes, they say that the Bible is good for a person's spiritual inspiration and comfort, but one cannot depend upon it for history. We believe that what God says in the historical books is of equal authority to that which is stated in any other part of the Bible. In his book, *The Inspiration of the Holy Scriptures,* Louis Gaussen points out that if it were allowable to place one book of God before another; we would "certainly give the preference to the historical books" (p. 287). He then presents several reasons for this assertion. The Penta-

---

[16] A. T. Pierson, *The Inspired Word* (South Nyack: Christian Alliance Publishing Company, n.d.), pp. 340, 341.
[17] Ryrie, "The Importance of Inerrancy," p. 141.

teuch of the Old Testament and the Gospels of the New—
historical books to be sure—are held in high esteem by the
Prophets and the Apostles. Christ quotes often from the
historical books of the Old Testament. These historical
books have been recorded and presented to us so that we
may know the facts concerning the character of God in His
dealings with men. The wise men of the ages never con-
ceived any view so magnificent as the doctrine of angels.
There is much about angelology in the historical books.
The historians who wrote the record were soldiers, priests,
tax-gatherers, shepherds, fishermen or kings. Yet what they
wrote concerning the doctrine of angels in the historical
books never conflicts with the remainder of Scripture. Biblical historians were also prophets for they recorded the
events which were for "our examples, to the intent we
should not lust after evil things, as they also lusted. . . Now
all these things happened unto them for ensamples [types]"
(1 Cor. 10:6, 11).

> If there be pages in the Bible that have need to be in-
> spired in every line and in every word, these are the
> historical books: they preach, they reveal, they set forth
> doctrine, they legislate, they prophesy. Compare them
> not, therefore, with other histories. They have quite
> another scope.[18]

If then, the historical books have such importance in
the divine revelation, and are quoted by the Son of God;
if they teach doctrines in harmony with, and never contra-
dicted by other scriptures; what man, professed theologian
or avowed atheist, has a right to belittle them by charging
them with inaccuracies and being nonessential?

Whatever God says is equally authoritative, regardless
of the book of the Bible where it is recorded. This is not to
say that all of God's words recorded in the Bible are of equal

---

[18] Louis Gaussen, *The Inspiration of the Holy Scripture* (Chicago:
Moody Press, 1949), pp. 292, 293.

importance. For example, in the Old Testament we have shadows of things to come; whereas in the New, we have the substance. Though the record of the sufferings of Job and Paul are as true as the record of the suffering of Jesus, no one would dare say that the sufferings of the first two were as important as the agonies of the suffering Savior. Not one word, chapter, book, or section of the Bible is unimportant. We cannot have a complete revelation without all of it, but the words pertaining to the soul's salvation are of more importance to our eternal welfare than are the words that describe the struggles in the Book of Judges.

Wherever the Bible speaks on a particular theme, it speaks truthfully and with equal authority. This position gives foundation to Biblical systematic theology. In order to know the whole of God's truth about a Biblical theme, we must discover what God says concerning it in every part of the Bible. What God says, for example, about the suffering Messiah in Isaiah 53 and Psalm 22 is equally necessary and authoritative with what is recorded in John 19. All records of the Bible dealing with any theme are factual, but when all of these facts on any theme are collated and systematized we have a complete and authoritative statement on the subject. Doctrine is based on fact.

> The authority which cannot assure of a hard fact is soon not trusted for a hard doctrine . . . . What we are to accept as the truth of God is a comparatively easy question if we can open our Bibles with the confident belief that what we read there is commended to us by a fully credible "Thus saith the Lord."[19]

D. AN AUTHORITY WHICH IS FINAL

We have sought to establish the point that the Bible is a credible, durable and united authority on every theme presented in its pages. Can we be sure, however, that new

---

[19] B. B. Warfield, *The Inspiration and Authority of the Bible* (Philadelphia: The Presbyterian and Reformed Publishing House, 1948), pp. 181, 182.

and different revelations may not be forthcoming, boasting the same claims? Since God inspired the record, is it logical to believe that He can and will reveal all the spiritual truth that His creature, man, will ever need in his journey on earth? An omniscient and omnipotent God Who has demonstrated His love to His people in so many ways would not fail to make known to them all truth necessary to their spiritual welfare. We believe, therefore, that the revelation presented in the Scriptures is both sufficient and final.

The finality of this revelation is brought into focus when we consider the warnings which God pronounces against those who add to it: "Ye shall not add unto the word which I command you, neither shall ye diminish ought from it. . ." (Deut. 4:2). "Every word of God is pure [refined]. . . Add thou not unto his words, lest he reprove thee, and thou be found a liar" (Prov. 30:5, 6). "For I testify to every man that heareth the words of the prophecy of this book, If any man shall add unto these things, God shall add unto him the plagues that are written in this book, And if any man shall take away from the words of the book of this prophecy, God shall take away his part out of the book of life. . ." (Rev. 22:18, 19). These are, indeed, solemn words found in the Law, the beginning of the Bible; the Proverbs in the middle of the Book; and in the Revelation, at the end of it. Tampering with the Word of God, either as the higher critics do when they take away from it, or as the false cults do when they add to it, is stated by God to be a serious matter and worthy of severe judgment.

In view of the finality of divine Biblical authority, adding to or taking from the revelation of God is not only prohibited by Him, but absolutely unnecessary. Some of us appreciate the old Puritan preacher who said, "There are just two things I desire to know: the first, does God speak? The second, what does God say?" He has spoken, and He has said enough to meet our spiritual needs all the way from the grace of God in salvation to the time when we shall have a glorified body in Heaven.

The psalmist said, "The law of the LORD is perfect. . ." (Psa. 19:7). ". . . All His commandments are sure" (Psa. 111:7). The Word of God has met man's needs down through the centuries of time, and nothing has been, or could be added to make it a better guide for His people.

> The Bible was completed more than eighteen centuries ago while the greater part of the world was uncivilized, and since John added the capstone to the Temple of God's Truth, there have been many wonderful discoveries, yet there have been no additions whatever to the moral or spiritual truths in it . . . . Through the centuries of the Christian era, man has succeeded in learning many of the secrets of nature, and has harnessed her forces to his service, but in the actual revelation of supernatural truth, nothing new has been discovered. Human writers cannot supplement the divine records for they are complete, entire, "wanting nothing."[20]

The fact that God ". . . hath in these last days spoken unto us by his Son. . ." (Heb. 1:1, 2) makes any so-called latter day revelation spurious by the very nature of their claims. If God has spoken, it is a final word; nothing else remains to be said. He has spoken by His Son, and His Son speaks through His written Word, the only authoritative record we have of His Person and work.

It has been argued that Christ is the authority unto Whom we should subject ourselves, and the Scripture is not the final word. He is presented as standing above and beyond the Word of God. He is the Judge of Scripture, we are told, and as His disciples we must judge it by Him in checking all which is not in harmony with His life and teaching.

---

[20] Emory H. Bancroft, *Christian Theology*, Revised edition (Grand Rapids: Zondervan Publishing House, 1961), p. 344.

But Who is this Christ, the Judge of the scriptures? Not the Christ of the New Testament and history: that Christ does not judge scripture, He obeys it and fulfills it by word and deed. He endorses the whole of it. Certainly, He is the final authority for Christians. That is precisely why Christians are bound to acknowledge the authority of scripture.[21]

If, as we claim, the Bible—the Word of God—is a credible, a durable, united and final authority, precisely what responsibility do we have to this inspired message? Jesus said, "If ye keep my commandments, ye shall abide in my love. . . Ye are my friends, if ye do whatsoever I command you" (John 15:10, 14). We must study the Word of God, know it, obey it, and pass on its wonderful message to others who need to hear it. The acceptance of Biblical inspiration, therefore, will make us students, dogmatists, servants and missionaries.

---

[21] Packer, *op. cit.,* p. 61.

II

THE IMPORTANCE OF INSPIRATION TO FULFILLED PROPHECY

The predictive element in the Scriptures is apparent even to the casual reader of the Bible. If there were only a few predictions which have been fulfilled, coincidence may explain them. According to one authority, there are over three hundred predictions of Christ in the Old Testament, most of which have already been fulfilled. A. T. Pierson refers to this prophetic element as "the eye of scripture with supernatural vision—backsight, insight, and foresight or power to see into the past, present and future."[22]

Attempts have been made to explain away the miraculous element in the prophetic predictions of the Bible. It has been said that predictive prophecy and the fulfillment were separated only by a short period of time; and the prophet, therefore, could have made a guess which fortunately came true.

---

[22] A. T. Pierson, *Knowing the Scriptures* (New York: Gospel Publishing House, 1910), p. 36.

The Septuagint version of the Old Testament, however, proves that the predictions were given hundreds of years before their fulfillment. This Greek translation of the Old Testament was brought into existence at least 215 years before the birth of Christ. The translation was begun in Alexandria in 285 B. C. Therefore, all the books of the Old Testament must be older since they had to be in existence to be translated. Who can look that far forward and predict with accuracy the events which the Bible declared would come to pass and have them so accurately fulfilled? Obviously, no one can do so apart from the Spirit of God Who knows the end from the beginning.

In challenging the false gods of Babylon, God caused Isaiah to write, "Produce your cause . . . shew us what shall happen . . . declare us things for to come . . . that we may know that ye are gods: yea, do good, or do evil, that we may be dismayed, and behold it together" (Isa. 41:21-23). Referring to Himself God said, "I am God, and there is none like me, Declaring the end from the beginning, and from ancient times the things that are not yet done, saying, My counsel shall stand, and I will do all my pleasure. . . I have spoken it, I will also bring it to pass; I have purposed it, I will also do it" (Isa. 46:9-11).

How can we explain these interesting and supernatural phenomena? The verbal inspiration of the prophetic predictions must be acknowledged since no man unaided by divine omniscience could record events which came to pass with such accuracy. Indeed, prophecy is history pre-written. Someone has said, "Prophecy is divine intervention in word, just as miracle is divine intervention in deed. The first reveals God's omniscience, the second His omnipotence."[23]

The prophecies in the Bible have been recorded by various writers in different contexts over a period covering many hundreds of years; but in spite of all the odds against

---

[23] George Henderson, *The Wonderful Word* (Covington, Kentucky: Calvary Book Room, n.d.), p. 109.

them, these prophecies have been, are being, or shall be literally fulfilled. Some of them have been entirely fulfilled literally. After the fall of Jericho, Joshua said, "Cursed be the man before the LORD, that riseth up and buildeth this city Jericho. . ." (Josh. 6:26). In 1 Kings 16:34, we read of the literal fulfillment of this prophecy. There are many other illustrations of this principle found in the Scriptures.

Other prophecies have been partially fulfilled literally. In Joel 2:28 through 32, we have the prediction which according to Acts 2:16 was partially fulfilled on the Day of Pentecost, and the Day of the Lord will fulfill the rest of it. When Jesus came to Nazareth, He went into the synagogue. When asked, He read from the prophecy of Isaiah. He made reference to Isaiah 61:1 through 3, and closed the reading with the reference to the "acceptable year of the Lord" (Luke 4:19) which was fulfilled when He came the first time. The rest of the prophecy, "the day of vengeance of our God," He did not read for the obvious reason that at that time it was yet future. (See also Dan. 9:25-27; Luke 1:31-33; Acts 2:29-36.) The literal fulfillment of a part of these Scriptures argues for the eventual literal fulfillment of the rest of them.

Since some prophecies have been completely fulfilled literally and others have been partially fulfilled literally, we have reason to believe that there are many prophecies which must have eventual fulfillment literally. We refer to such great prophetic events as the literal return of Christ (John 14:1-4; Acts 1:1-11); the Rapture of the saints (1 Thess. 4:13-17); the resurrection of the dead (1 Cor. 15:52, 53); and the literal reign of the Lord on the earth (Rev. 20:1-6). This truth ought to have practical application to us now for the God Who fulfills His prophecy will most certainly keep His promises which He has given for our daily blessing and enjoyment (Jer. 33:3; Heb. 13:5; 1 John 5:14).

Too many divine predictions have already been fulfilled to place them in the realm of fortunate guesses making them mere coincidences and the product of human wisdom.

> A great mathematician once said that the accidental fulfillment of the prophecies of the Bible which have been accurately and precisely accomplished might be compared to a fraction whose numerator is a single grain of sand, and whose denominator is the bulk of the earth many times magnified.[24]

God has declared things to come. He has dealt with the beginning and the end of many interesting and important things in between. Though there are many areas of prophetic study which show the importance of inspiration to fulfilled prophecy, we limit our observation to four.

A. THE JEWISH NATION

The fact that there are Jews in the world today is beyond explanation apart from the providential care of God. No other nation has been so persecuted and driven to and fro upon the face of the earth and survived. These people have been hated, despised, slaughtered, and in many ways caused to suffer; yet as a distinct race they live on.

About 2,000 B.C. God gave a promise to Abraham assuring him that He would make his seed "as the dust of the earth" (Gen. 13:16). When the promise was given, both Abraham and his wife were old. They had neither son, nor the human possibility of ever having one. Today, however, it is estimated that there are twelve million Jews in the world. Surely, God alone gave the promise, and the Holy Spirit inspired the writing.

The prophecies which relate to this ancient people are so interwoven and detailed that divine omniscience alone

---

[24] G. Day, *op. cit.*, p. 52.

can account for them. The Bible predicts the rejection of the Messiah by this nation to whom He was particularly sent (Isa. 49:7; 53:3). The Jews were educated to expect and identify the coming Messiah, but when "He came unto his own . . . his own received him not" (John 1:11). Though they should have been able to identify Him, they crucified Him. Since they were looking for a Messiah of might and power, this crucifixion itself proves to the Jewish mind that His claims as their Messiah are invalid. They do not identify the prophecies of the suffering servant in Isaiah 53 with Christ. There are many other prophecies in the Old Testament which predict this rejection (Psa. 118:22; Isa. 30:9-12). Though the rejection of the Messiah might at first appear to be a proof against Christianity, it is one of its strongest evidences. He was rejected as predicted, and therefore the Word of God is substantiated as an authority.

Many of the Jewish people have read the Old Testament and know that their rejection of the Messiah was predicted. Why has Israel not turned from this state of rejection then, since this message has been sounded into Jewish ears for almost nineteen centuries? If their rejection of the Word of God has demonstrated that this message is true, why hasn't this nation turned to God? This the Jews have not done. In fact, the rejection of the Messiah is as pronounced now as it was in the beginning years of the Christian era. This continued rejection, rather than weakening the argument for an infallible Bible, further strengthens it. This prolonged and determined rejection of the Messiah was also predicted. In Isaiah 6:9 through 12, the rejection is prophesied. The prophet asks, "Lord, how long?" The answer is given: "Until the cities be wasted without inhabitant, and the houses without man, and the land be utterly desolate, And the Lord have removed men far away, and there be a great forsaking in the midst of the land." The New Testament counterpart to this is found in Romans

11:25, "Blindness [hardness] in part is happened to Israel, until the fulness of the Gentiles be come in." Paul indicates here that the hardness will continue until He selects out of the Gentiles a people for His name (Acts 15:14). Thus the rejection continues to the present time and beyond it.

Moses on the way to the Promised Land told Israel, "The LORD shall scatter thee among all people, from the one end of the earth even unto the other . . . no ease . . . neither . . . rest: but . . . a trembling heart . . . failing of eyes . . . sorrow of mind . . . thou shalt fear day and night . . ." (Deut. 28:64-66). This universal dispersion of the Jews has been in the process of fulfillment through many centuries as they have been scattered and persecuted in Assyria, Babylon, Rome, Spain, Greece, Poland, Russia and Germany. Who but God could have foretold these sad experiences for the people who were the "apple of His eye" and His "peculiar treasure"?

Another amazing fact that we must not overlook is that these people were not only dispersed according to prophecy, but their preservation was also predicted. "And yet for all that, when they be in the land of their enemies, I will not cast them away, neither will I abhor them, to destroy them utterly, and to break my covenant with them: for I am the LORD their God" (Lev. 26:44).

> That a nation deprived of its fatherland, wandering over all the earth, without any home or rallying place, deprived, too, of the chief ceremonies and institutions of the religion which had been the main instrument in binding them together as a people—that a nation so placed should not be absorbed by the peoples among whom they sojourned, and should not disappear as a distinct and separate race is contrary to reason and experience.[25]

---

[25] John Urquhart, *The Wonders of Prophecy* (New York: Christian Publishing Company, n.d.), p. 229.

The Jewish people could not be a part of the nations if they wanted to. They must continue as a separate people. "And that which cometh into your mind shall not be at all, that ye say, We will be as the heathen, as the families of the countries, to serve wood and stone" (Ezek. 20:32). Their idolatrous practices, unbelievable persecutions, nor plans which they sought to make would enable them to blot out their own distinctives which so obviously differentiate them from the nations. Through history they run as a separate stream in the ocean of humanity. The Mississippi River may carry mud far out into the Gulf of Mexico, but eventually the water becomes a part of the sea. This has not happened, nor will it happen to Israel though it has run for many years into the sea of humanity. This nation has been preserved for centuries without a central government, sacrifice, or voice from God. "For the children of Israel shall abide many days without a king, and without a prince, and without a sacrifice, and without an image, and without an ephod, and without teraphim" (Hos. 3:4). In the next verse, however, we have a reference to their restoration for the prophet continues, "Afterward shall the children of Israel return, and seek the LORD their God. . . ." In another place God's promise is given, "I will bring thy seed from the east . . . the west . . . the north . . . the south . . . from the ends of the earth . . . from all the nations" (Isa. 43:5, 6; Jer. 29:14). God scattered them to the ends of the earth and will also bring them back from the same remote spots. That the way has been opened for this fulfillment one can see as one reads contemporary history. The League of Nations made Palestine a British mandate, and the British Balfour Declaration guaranteed a national home for the Jewish people. Other facts of history will show fulfillment of these prophecies. In our time God is in the process of fulfilling His Word concerning His ancient people. We are thus living in the day when before our very eyes the prophetic Scriptures are being fulfilled. Though it is impossible now to declare dogmatically that Israel's presence in the land is secure until the return of Christ, her Messiah, she is in the land as a nation for the first time in more than two thousand years.

B. THE ANCIENT CITIES

Though there are a number of instances in the Bible where predictions were made concerning ancient cities and history records the fulfillment thereof, we cite only a few to illustrate again the importance of verbal inspiration to Biblical prophecy.

Tyre and Sidon are two cities of great interest because the prophecies concerning them are so different even though they are located in the same general area. Concerning Tyre, Ezekiel records the following prophecy:

> Behold, I am against thee, O Tyrus, and will cause many nations to come up against thee, as the sea causeth his waves to come up. And they shall destroy the walls of Tyrus, and break down her towers: I will also scrape her dust from her, and make her like the top of a rock. It shall be a place for the spreading of nets in the midst of the sea: for I have spoken it, saith the Lord GOD: and it shall become a spoil to the nations. . . And they shall make a spoil of thy riches, and make a prey of thy merchandise: and they shall break down thy walls, and destroy thy pleasant houses: and they shall lay thy stones and thy timber and thy dust in the midst of the water (Ezek. 26:3-5, 12) .

The city of Tyre was besieged for some thirteen years, and by its powerful fleet it was able to repel its enemies. But in the sixth century B. C., it was taken by Nebuchadnezzar. He destroyed Tyre, and it was never rebuilt. Some of the refugees, however, took cover on an island about one-half mile from the mainland. Here, a second Tyre was built.

The ruins of the city still stood. For two and a half

centuries after Nebuchadnezzar's destruction the predictions
in Ezekiel 26:12 were left unfulfilled. Alexander the Great,
then in his power, expressed a desire to worship in the city
of Tyre. The inhabitants of this island city of Tyre knew
what this would mean. Alexander would come to worship,
but would stay to master. His armies marched through the
old city of Tyre—about a half-mile away from the city they
came to attack. How could he reach this island? He con-
structed a causeway using the "walls . . . houses . . . stones . . .
timber . . . dust" as material for his bridge from the mainland to the island city. So great was the demand for the
material that even the dust was used and the old city became like a "top of a rock" (v. 14).

Suppose the Old Testament prophecies were "created"
for effect, and were not recorded sufficiently far removed
from the fulfillment to give reason to believe that they were
miraculously recorded. Not all the prediction (Ezek. 26:13,
14) was fulfilled when Nebuchadnezzar conquered the mainland city, nor even when Alexander the Great took the
island city. The Bible says, "Thou shalt be built no more."
Urquhart says, "The site remains today without even a
mound to mark it. It has to be determined solely by the
notices in ancient writers which give its distance from the
island Tyre."[26]

Now let us consider the prophecies pronounced upon
the city of Sidon. "Thus saith the Lord God: Behold, I
am against thee, O Zidon; and I will be glorified in the
midst of thee: and they shall know that I am the Lord,
when I shall have executed judgments in her, and shall be
sanctified in her. For I will send into her pestilence, and
blood into her streets; and the wounded shall be judged in
the midst of her by the sword upon her on every side; and
they shall know that I am the Lord" (Ezek. 28: 22, 23).
Pestilence and blood are promised. The prophecy that the

---

[26] *Ibid.,* p. 19.

city will be built no more is absent. There is no predicted doom of extinction pronounced against this city. Under Persian dominion when Tyre was deserted, Sidon was a great city. It rebelled under Artaxerxes Ochus, and the pressure against it became unbearable. When all hope was gone forty thousand citizens shut themselves up in their dwellings and set fire to them. Some of the citizens of the city were absent at the time of this holocaust. Upon their return they rebuilt the city. During the Crusades the city was taken many times and great destruction was wrought upon it. Through the years it has been taken by a number of nations. In 1840 it was bombarded by the combined fleets of England, Austria and Turkey. It has been taken, sacked, bombarded, burned, and otherwise destroyed, but always rebuilt.

Finally, consider Jerusalem in the light of prophecy. "That saith of Cyrus, He is my shepherd, and shall perform all my pleasure: even saying unto Jerusalem, Thou shalt be built; and to the temple, Thy foundations shall be laid" (Isa. 44:28). Some 150 years before Cyrus was born this prophecy was recorded by Isaiah. His name was given and his actions so unlike those of a pagan emperor were described. This certainly takes this prediction out of the realm of coincidence and places it in a sphere of supernatural revelation.

In another place Isaiah said, "As birds flying, so will the LORD of hosts defend Jerusalem; defending also he will deliver it; and passing over he will preserve it" (Isa. 31:5). It has been suggested that this prophecy was fulfilled some 2,600 years later when General Allenby took the city of Jerusalem from the Turks during the first World War.

How can we account for the treatment of these cities? Why are the prophecies so accurate and so precisely fulfilled?

There is one explanation in which alone, far though it takes us, the mind will rest with perfect satisfaction.

It is that He speaks here Whose thought grasps the ages, and before Whom the future has no veil and Who in these proofs of His faithfulness writes on man's heart the assurance "Heaven and earth shall pass away, but My Word shall not pass away."[27]

C. THE PROMISED MESSIAH

It has been said that there are over three hundred predictions in the Old Testament concerning Christ which find fulfillment in the New. "The nature of the Redeemer's work and even His character in history are so minutely described that it is possible to compile a history of Christ and Christianity merely from the prophecies."[28] We ought not to be amazed at Old Testament predictions since Christ Himself said, ". . .The scriptures . . . testify of me" (Luke 4:17, 18; 24:27; John 5:39). Truly "the testimony of Jesus is the spirit of prophecy" (Rev. 19:10). Christ is the Key which unlocks the prophetic Scriptures. "All prophecy is to find application and fulfillment in the past sufferings, present sufficiency, and future sovereignty of the Lord Jesus."[29]

The fact that so many Old Testament Scriptures refer to Christ and have been fulfilled exactly as foretold bears evidence to the importance of verbal inspiration of the prophetic Word. Had God not selected the words for the prophets to say, they could not have chosen their own unaided by Him and thus have written so accurately.

In order to see how precisely the Old Testament portrays the coming of Christ, we can consider a few of the many Scriptures relating to the main events or crises of Christ.

1. HIS BIRTH

The Bible predicted that He would come from the nation of Israel (Num. 24:17; Luke 1:31); of the tribe of

---

[27] *Ibid.,* p. 21.
[28] *Ibid.,* p. 200.
[29] Lehman Strauss, *God's Plan For The Future* (Grand Rapids: Zondervan Publishing House, 1965), pp. 10, 27.

Judah (Gen. 49:10; Heb. 7:14); of the seed of Abraham (Gen. 12:3; Gal. 3:8); of the seed of the woman (Gen. 3:15; Gal. 4:4); born of a virgin mother without a human father (Isa. 7:14; Mat. 1:23); to be called Immanuel (Isa. 7:14; Matt. 1:22, 23); to be born in Bethlehem (Mic. 5:2; Matt. 2:5, 6). If these predictions were not inspired by the Holy Spirit, each additional definite statement multiplied the possibility of exposure; but each of the details listed here has been fulfilled; therefore, the supernatural element in the Scriptures must be accepted by any honest, open-minded person.

2. HIS LIFE

Prophets foretold that He would be preserved from the hatred of men (Hos. 11:1; Matt. 2:15); rejected by His own brothers (Psa. 69:8; Matt. 8:20; John 7:5); and confound the wise men in the temple (Psa. 119:99; Luke 2:46, 47).

3. HIS MINISTRY

Long before our Savior began to serve on earth, His ministry was announced as beginning in Galilee (Isa. 9:1, 2; Matt. 4:12, 16-23); characterized by miracles (Isa. 35:5, 6; Matt. 11:4-6; Luke 7:22); while His teaching was to be illustrated by parables (Psa. 78:2, 4; Matt. 13:34, 35). His message though clearly presented was to be rejected by the Jews (Isa. 6:9, 10; Matt. 13:14, 15). Though born of a kingly line, His poverty was also predicted (Isa. 53:2; Luke 9:58). He did not come among men parading certain advantages. They said of Him, "How knoweth this man letters, having never learned?" (John 7:15). He had no promise of worldly gain to offer His followers. Said He, "Foxes have holes, and the birds of the air have nests; but the Son of man hath not where to lay his head" (Luke 9:58).

The Old Testament predicts that He would be persecuted and patiently endure it (Isa. 53:7; Acts 8:32-35); He was to be hated without a cause (Psa. 69:4; John 15:25);

betrayed by a friend (Psa. 41:9; Matt. 26:50; John 13:18); and deserted by His disciples (Zech. 13:7; Matt. 26:31).

4. HIS DEATH

Through the guidance of the Holy Spirit, many Old Testament writers gave descriptive pictures of the Savior's death and the events which led up to it. He was rejected by His own (Isa. 49:7; 53:3; John 1:11); betrayed (Psa. 41:9; John 18:8); falsely accused (Psa. 35:11; Mark 14:56); but silent to His accusers (Isa. 53:7; Matt. 27:12-14). The record continues to describe His treatment in the hands of His enemies by pointing out that He was to be smitten (Isa. 53:6; Matt. 26:67); nailed to the cross (Psa. 22:16; John 19:18); marred (Isa. 52:14; John 19:5); spat upon (Isa. 53:5; Matt. 26:67); and crucified between two thieves (Isa. 53:12; Matt. 27:38); while on the cross He was to be given gall to drink (Psa. 69:21; Matt. 27:34); and pierced with a spear (Zech. 12:10; John 19:34). He is pictured on the Cross dying as One forsaken while around Him they were gambling for His garments (Psa. 22:18; John 19:24). In spite of His ill-treatment, not a bone was to be broken (Exod. 12:46; John 19:36). His death in the Old Testament as well as the New is pictured as voluntary and vicarious (Psa. 40:6-8; John 10:17, 18). Through all of this His disciples were to be scattered after the Crucifixion (Zech. 13:7; Matt. 26:31); while His body was buried with the rich (Isa. 53:9; Matt. 27:57-60). The death of Christ has more prophetic description than any other event in His earthly ministry. Psalm 22 gives twenty and Isaiah 53 gives approximately thirty prophecies of His crucifixion. The gospel record shows the literal fulfillment of all of them.

5. HIS ASCENSION

The Old Testament clearly predicts the resurrection of Jesus Christ from the dead (Psa. 16:9, 10; Acts 2:27-31); prophets saw Him ascending into Heaven (Psa. 16:11; 68:18;

Acts 1:9; 2:32; 2:36); and restored to His former glory (Exod. 24:10-17; John 17:1, 4, 5).

6. His Return

The Old Testament has much to say about the Second Coming of Christ. The prophets declare that He will return (Deut. 33:2; Jude 14, 15) to judge (Isa. 53:2; Thess. 1:8); and to set up His kingdom (Psa. 96:13; Isa. 1:26; 2 Tim. 4:1). The prophecies of His first advent were fulfilled with absolute literalness. We can expect, therefore, that the prophecies of His second advent will be fulfilled in the same literal sense.

The Word of God is accurate in its predictions. These prophecies were recorded by a number of individual writers over many years, and in most cases without knowledge of what the others penned; yet there is precision in detail. There are at least thirty-three prophecies which were fulfilled in one day when Jesus died. In the light of these facts we must conclude that the Bible is verbally inspired by God to so precisely portray the coming of the Messiah hundreds of years before He appeared.

It is not only true that Christ is the main Theme of prophecy; He is also the Prophet. To Moses God said, "I will raise them up a Prophet from among their brethren, like unto thee, and will put my words in his mouth; and he shall speak unto them all that I shall command him" (Deut. 18:18). The woman of Sychar knew that such a Prophet was expected (John 4:25). Christ made it clear that He was the One in Whose mouth the Father had put His words. "As my Father hath taught me, I speak these things" (John 8:28). "I have not spoken of myself . . . the Father . . . sent me . . . gave me a commandment, what I should say, and what I should speak" (John 12:49 cf. 17:8).

Christ was not only a Prophet in the sense of telling forth as is evident in His sermons, but He was a Prophet Who foretold future events. The parables of Matthew 13 combine both aspects of the prophetic office as it refers to Christ. For example, the sowing of the seed shows how His Word is received by various hearers in the present (13:3-9). The parable of the tares declares future judgment on the basis of present actions (13:24-30, 36-43). At least six whole chapters (Matt. 24, 25; Mark 13; Luke 21; John 14, 16), in the Gospels are prophetic utterances of Christ. He is, indeed, both the Theme and the Prophet of Biblical prophecy. He is thus demonstrated to be the unique Son of God for no one else could speak as He did, and the Scriptures are demonstrated to be the Word of God for only divine revelation could predict His coming as they do.

D. THE WORLD CONDITIONS

The prophetic Scriptures indicate that intellectual, religious, governmental, physical and psychological phenomena shall prevail at the end of the age. In Luke's account of the Olivet discourse, Christ the Prophet made reference to each of these signs when He said, "Take heed that ye be not deceived . . . many shall come in my name, saying, I am *Christ* . . . Nation shall rise against nation . . . great earthquakes shall be in divers places . . . Men's hearts failing them for fear . . ." (Luke 21:8, 10, 26). These predictions are made and interpreted as proof of verbal inspiration, for Jesus said, "Heaven and earth shall pass away: but my words shall not pass away" (v. 33).

There is an abundance of scriptural evidence to prove that the man of sin shall come on the world scene; that men shall hate one another on an international scale demonstrated in wars; that the divine institutions of home, church and government shall gradually disintegrate and reap the judgment of God as the only means of correction. Why is all this inevitable? Why should it come to pass when the human race is ever learning and "knowledge shall be increased" (Dan. 12:4)? Cannot men do something to offset or correct these terrible conditions?

Paul gives the answer to these questions in 2 Timothy 3:1 through 7. Here we have clearly stated a description of the character or inner life of mankind at the end of the age. Wars will prevail, divine institutions shall be rejected and Antichrist will be readily accepted because of what the human race will be morally at the end of the age.

There are five Greek words in this passage of Scripture which describe man in the perilous times of the last days. Each of them has as its basis the word *phileo,* which means "to love, regard with affection, to like, to be fond of, to manifest some act or token of kindness." These five words appear as a summary of the other characteristics of the last days as described by Paul in this somewhat neglected eschatological passage.

1. Philautoi, "self-lovers." Men shall be without natural affection, boasters, high-minded or puffed up, or one who shows himself to be above other people. Essentially, human beings act as they do because they are selfish. They are selfish because they are sinful. The natural man's desires, plans and motives are all centered in himself as he becomes less and less dependent upon God. This is evident in a successive study of these words.

2. Philarguroi, "money-lovers." The word is used only here; in Luke 16:13 and 14, "Ye cannot serve God and mammon. And the Pharisees also, who were covetous . . . derided him"; and in 1 Timothy 6:10, ". . . The love of money is the root of all evil. . . ." Essentially, those who are self-lovers will become money-lovers. Some depraved souls in our day will do anything for money. Thus, we have an increase in the crime rate and almost uncontrolled delinquency problems. All of us must be on guard because of the "deceitfulness of riches" (Matt. 13:22).

3. Aphilagathoi, "holding no fondness for either good *men* or good *things.*" This is a negative word which sums up the other negatives in the text such as disobedient, unthankful, unholy, incontinent, etc. It means to lack concern for the things which are true, honest, just, pure, lovely, of good report—which are the good things every Christian earnestly seeks. The word describes the lowering of moral standards and the new morality of our time.

4. Philedonai, "pleasure-lovers." This term describes those who seek for the gratifying of the natural or sinful desires. Paul refers to it as "serving divers lusts and pleasures . . ." (Titus 3:3). James says this is the cause of "wars" (or brawlings) among the people because their "lusts" (or pleasures) war in their members. Some would rather apply this word "pleasure-lovers" to acts of worldliness, but the indignity of the scriptural application to church fights was emphasized. Worldliness is not necessarily a series of acts, but a heart attitude. The word "heady" in the context gives an illustration of *philedonai.* Vincent describes this person as one who is "precipitate, reckless, headstrong in the pursuit of a bad end under the influence of passion."[30]

5. Philotheoi, "God-lovers." The "more than" preceding the word gives it a negative meaning. Those who are self-lovers eventually become those who are not God-lovers. "Blasphemers . . . unthankful, unholy" are other words in the text which describe this attitude. This is a sin of the religious, for the reference is to those having a "form of godliness, but denying the power thereof. . . ." When men who should love God love their lust more, what can be said of those who make no profession of Him whatsoever? Today there seems to be more interest in the god of human achievement than in the God of the Bible. Daniel predicted that the coming man of sin shall "honour the god of forces . . ." (Dan. 11:38). We need not wonder then at a world which will bow to a man "Who opposeth and

---

[30] Marvin R. Vincent, *Word Studies in the New Testament,* Vol. IV (New York: Charles Scribner's Sons, 1905), p. 311.

exalteth himself above all that is called God . . ." (2 Thess. 2:4). A "fierce" (2 Tim. 3:3) or "uncivilized" world will not be in love with the God of the Bible, but will wholly follow the god of the world.

Dr. Patrick Fairbairn, in *The Pastoral Epistles* published in 1874 commenting on this passage, wrote:

> It is a very dreadful picture, and from the very darkness of the characteristics it delineates, it plainly requires to be understood with some limitations. If such characteristics were to become general in any particular age or country, society could not long continue to exist. It would fall to pieces by the weight of its own corruptions.[31]

One wonders how Fairbairn would write upon this Scripture if he were alive today! We must observe that "the end shall not be yet."

How could Paul write so accurately about a period of time so far ahead of his own day and beyond the comprehensions of theologians who lived one hundred years ago, yet obviously being fulfilled in part at least in our time? The answer is obvious. Paul recorded the words which the Holy Spirit directed him to pen. This prophecy, unfulfilled or in the process of being fulfilled today, must be placed with other fulfilled prophecies as evidence of the verbal, plenary inspiration of the Scriptures.

---

[31] Patrick Fairbairn, *The Pastoral Epistles* (Edinburgh: T. & T. Clark, 1874), p. 365.

III

THE IMPORTANCE OF INSPIRATION TO THE EXPOSITORY PREACHER

It makes a great deal of difference whether or not a preacher believes in the verbal, plenary inspiration of the Scriptures. The ministry of one who accepts the Bible as the authority will have far different aims and results than those of a man who bases his preaching on the great thoughts of other men. If the Bible is not God's Word, then it is only at best the thinking of good men and compares at the best only favorably with other good writings which human genius has produced. If, on the other hand, it is the Word of God in its entirety, then a God-called preacher is under orders to preach it entirely. This can be done only by expository preaching. The preacher who engages in this type of ministry is described in Psalm 1:2 and 3. He must delight in the Word of God and meditate therein constantly. As a result his ministry will be like the fruit from the tree planted by the rivers of water. Thus relating the preacher to his preaching, F. B. Meyer defined expository preaching as "the consecutive treatment of some book or extended portion of Scripture on which the preacher has concentrated head and heart, brain and brawn, over which he has thought and wept and prayed until it has yielded up its inner secret and the spirit of it has passed into his spirit."[32] The Biblical view of inspiration when accepted by the preacher will make his ministry one of power.

A. IT AFFECTS HIS INTERPRETATION BY GIVING HIM COMPREHENSION

One who accepts the whole Bible as divine authority takes for granted that though there is diversity in the record because God used the personalities of the writers, there is unity of meaning since the Holy Spirit authored the entire revelation. All of the Scripture testimony on any subject must be considered if we are to arrive at the whole truth. Peter stated this principle when he wrote, ". . . No prophecy of the scripture is of any private interpretation" (2 Pet. 1:20).

Discounting verbal inspiration, the preacher has a book akin to *Poor Richard's Almanac* which gives him a long series of isolated and somewhat scattered proverbs; but he does not have a book from which he can ascertain the mind of God.

To understand the Bible, the preacher must believe in verbal inspiration. "Apart from inspiration embracing the words of scripture, there could be no exegetical study of the Bible."[33] Inspiration extends to the significance of a phrase as the "Yet once more" in Hebrews 12:27; the inviolability of a single word as "gods" in John 10:34 through 36; the use of a single letter as in the plural "seeds" in Galatians 3:16; the voice of the verb "known" in Galatians

---

[32] F. B. Meyer, *Expository Preaching* (London: Hodder and Stoughton, n.d.), p. 29.
[33] Unger, *op. cit.*, p. 432.

4:9; and the importance of a tense, as "Before Abraham was, I am" in John 8:58.

Because the Bible is in its entirety the Word of God, there are certain principles or laws which have meaning to the Bible student as he seeks to understand its message. In order to show the importance of inspiration to the understanding of the Bible, reference is made to four of them.

1. THE PRINCIPLE OF FIRST MENTION

It is of interest to observe that the first mention of a doctrine in the Bible seems to be the key to understanding its meaning in the rest of Scripture. Since the Bible was penned by many different writers we can account for this principle of interpretation only by divine inspiration of each verse. Otherwise, the meaning of a word would likely be different in the various references if the Bible were a book of many authors.

> Whenever any person, place, important word, or subject is first referred to in scripture, all subsequent recurrence of the same is forecast or hinted so that such first glimpse indicates its relation to the entire testimony and teaching of scripture. The Spirit of God thus supplies in such primary mention a clue to all that follows on the same topic.[34]

There are many examples in the Scriptures of this law. We cite only a few for illustration. The word *grace* is defined in its first mention (Gen. 6:8). The word is used in the context of divine judgment. One man, Noah, who as a sinner deserves only judgment, is saved by grace through faith and does not reap this condemnation because of his trust in God (Rom. 4:16; 11:6; Heb. 11:7). He received God's favor when he deserved God's wrath. The word *sanctified* found in Genesis 2:3 is another word which is defined by its first mention. God sets apart the seventh

---

day as a day of rest; therefore, we understand that the word *sanctify* means to *separate* or *set apart* anything or anyone for some higher use or purpose. Since there is no such thing as a "sinless day," the first mention of sanctification cannot refer to sinless perfection.

The same principle operates in relation to expressions found in the Bible. Christ is referred to as the *Son of Man* in Psalm 8:4 through 6. This is a prophetic reference to Him when He shall take dominion of the earth, and is so used in other parts of the Scripture. The *day of the Lord,* mentioned twenty-four times in the Bible, is found first in Isaiah 2:11 and 12, and gives us the key to its meaning. It refers to the time of man's humiliation: "The lofty looks of man shall be humbled"; and the exaltation of God: "The LORD alone shall be exalted in that day." The *day of the Lord* used elsewhere in the Bible has this two-fold application.

2. THE PRINCIPLE OF PROGRESSIVE MENTION

The Holy Spirit Who inspired the Scriptures does not reveal the whole meaning of a thing all at once. The truth is progressively revealed through a series of references, thus to have the whole truth one must have the whole Bible.

> If from the first to the last reference to a subject, the intermediate mention of it is traced, there will be found often, if not always, an advance from what is rudimental and fundamental to what is higher and completer; but which can only be understood when first principles have been taught; so that when the last mention is reached, it is like placing the capstone upon a building.[35]

There are many illustrations of this principle in the Bible. The Lamb of God is typified in Genesis 4:4; provided in Genesis 22:8; killed for the first time in Exodus 12:1 through12; personified in Isaiah 53:7; identified in John

---

[35] *Ibid.,* p. 260.

1:29; magnified in Revelation 5:6; and glorified in Revelation 21:23. The whole truth about the Lamb of God is not known by any single reference, but becomes clearer as the Revelation progresses. Peter gathers all the teaching together in one summarizing statement which we find in 1 Peter 1:18 through 21.

> Here is a steady progress without a single check or break from Genesis 4 to Revelation 22 about the Lamb. Every new stage of treatment adds something to what has gone before and that has not been mentioned which prepares for something that is coming after that, otherwise we are not able to understand it.[36]

If this principle is not observed, how can a Bible preacher understand all facets of a Bible subject? He must believe in the verbal, plenary inspiration of the Scriptures in order for this principle to have any significance.

3. The Principle of Comparative Mention

A study of the Bible reveals that certain passages may be placed side by side and complement one another or show decided contrast. A. T. Pierson suggests that we may place Bible verses in this position.

> First, for the purpose of comparing them as to the things in which they resemble each other; and second, to compare them in things in which they are unlike and learn a lesson from contrast; and third, to see how one adds to and completes or complements that which is contained in the others.[37]

The parable of the talents (Matt. 25:14-30) and the pounds (Luke 19:11-27) have enough dissimilarities to show that they do not refer to the same incident. There are enough similarities, however, to teach God's principle of

---

[36] A. T. Pierson, *The Bible and Spiritual Criticism* (London: James Nisbet & Company, 1906), p. 157.

[37] *Ibid.*, pp. 55, 56.

reward; and in this fashion these parables complement each other.

In Ephesians 5:19 we are commanded to be filled with the Holy Spirit. In Colossians 3:15, the believer is instructed to let the Word of Christ dwell in him. In these two texts almost the same language is used to describe similar results. When we put the two together we discover that no man is filled with the Spirit who is not filled with, controlled by, and obedient to the Word of God. The Biblical preacher finds meaning in these and many other scriptural comparisons because he believes the words of the Bible are inspired and have distinct meaning in their use and relation one with the other.

4. The Principle of Full Mention

Subjects vital to our spiritual welfare are given full treatment in some specific section of the Scripture. "It is very natural that if there be one speaker behind the various books in the Word of God, He should once for all somewhere declare to us his full mind upon any subject vital to our spiritual life."[38] It would be difficult to find any major subject in the Bible with a specific relationship to our spiritual life which does not have a "full mention" somewhere in the Holy Writ.

In the Old Testament, Exodus 20 gives full treatment to the Ten Commandments; Psalm 119 reveals the perfection of the Word of God; Isaiah 53 declares the vicarious sacrifice of Christ. In the New Testament, the Gospel of John gives full treatment to a number of subjects: John 3 is a complete treatment to regeneration; John 4 gives the meaning of the Water of Life; John 6 identifies the Bread of Life; John 14 deals with Heaven; John 17 teaches the meaning of intercessory prayer by the example of Christ.

In other sections of the New Testament we find rather exhaustive treatment of such things as the laws of the

---

[38] *Ibid.*, p. 45.

kingdom in Matthew 5:7; God's love for the lost, Luke 15; and a complete commentary on the end of the age recorded in Matthew 24 and 25. The God-Man is presented in Hebrews 1 and 2. The resurrection of the body is given rather complete treatment in 1 Corinthians 15. The doctrine of God's love through the believer is defined in 1 Corinthians 13, and a commentary on faith is recorded in Hebrews 11.

Let it be emphasized once again that without these and other related principles of interpretation, the Bible will be a book of rather confused statements. Apart from the verbal, plenary inspiration of the Scriptures these rules of interpretation have no meaning nor basis for use since the Bible would be a composite of many books authored by men without any unifying relationship to one another.

B. IT AFFECTS HIS PREPARATION BY GIVING HIM CONTENT

Paul charged Timothy to "Preach the word. . ." (2 Tim. 4:2). This commission was given within the context of what Paul taught concerning the approaching apostasy (2 Tim. 3:1-8) and the true nature of the Word of God (Tim. 3:16). The "Word" means more than the "gospel," although the gospel is included in it, of course. It is "all the counsel of God" (Acts 20:27).

The preacher who believes that "All scripture is given by inspiration of God" will of necessity prepare sermons that are:

1. RICH IN CONTENT

He will bring content into his sermons from a supply which is inexhaustible. Early in one's ministry he may become frustrated when thinking of the preparation of the two inevitable sermons for Sunday and another Bible study for prayer meeting. Later on he will discover that a lifetime will not be long enough to preach all the material the Bible supplies. "The man who reads it (the Bible) for the first time is struck by the force of its evident truths, but he who reads it for the 100th time is awed by its vast imponderables."[39]

Sermon content will be rich for one who practices Biblical preaching. The more he takes out of the Bible the more there seems to be left in it.

> The preacher who will honor the Word of God by believing that it has unity and coherence, that it actually unfolds the divine plan and purpose from eternity past to eternity future, and who diligently studies it in this attitude of reverent faith, will be more and more amazed at its wonders and find himself possessed of an ever-increasing store of thrilling and heart-warming truth which will furnish the basis of more sermons than he could preach in a lifetime.[40]

As the years go by the man of God will discover that there are depths in this Book which he cannot fathom. This knowledge of his source of supply gives him a great appreciation for the Bible and a reverence in his study of it. He knows this Book reveals God, and exclaims with Paul, "O the depth of the riches both of the wisdom and knowledge of God! how unsearchable are his judgments, and his ways past finding out!" (Rom. 11:33). In the revelation of God one must expect a Book of inexhaustible depths. "The more men have pondered the Bible the more aware they have become of the limitless, incomprehensible quality. Such is true of no other book ever written."[41]

2. DOCTRINAL IN CONTENT

The expository preacher will, of necessity, be a doctrinal preacher. Because he believes in verbal inspiration he will study to be sure the words and terms of Holy Writ are defined. The inspired Word is, indeed, ". . . profit-

---

[39] G. Day, *op. cit.,* p. 195.
[40] Merrill F. Unger, *Principles of Expository Preaching* (Grand Rapids: Zondervan Publishing House, 1955), p. 270.
[41] G. Day, *op. cit.,* p. 191.

able for doctrine" (2 Tim. 3:16). Doctrine is another word for teaching. One of the preacher's objectives will be the impartation of information to his hearers. This will involve Biblical facts and clear definition of terms that can only be obtained by a thorough study of the Bible itself.

The Bible places a great deal of emphasis upon doctrine (John 16:7-16; Rom. 6:17; Eph. 4:14; 2 Tim. 3:16). "Every expositor must have a theology. The reason for this is obvious. Since the Bible is the revelation of God's truth, any serious study of it must lead to the foundation of doctrines."[42]

Serious study of large sections of chapters and books of the Bible, and the constant teaching of them will help to keep the preacher from building his doctrine on human philosophy and speculation. The content of the expository sermon will always be Biblical, even though it may deal with topics currently related to the philosophies and problems of the day.

3. BALANCED IN CONTENT

The expository ministry will have a balance unknown by the topical, textual, or extra-biblical preaching. It will teach *all* that the Bible has to say on a subject, and *only* what it says. It will reveal facts and not speculative ideas.

In a balanced expository ministry, one will avoid two extremes, both of which often brings Bible preaching of a textual or topical method into ill repute. One extreme is the failure to deal with all the revealed facts in a Bible passage or is the temptation to let curiosity lead to shallow, superficial preaching found in the ministry which fails or refuses to deal with the great doctrines of the faith. The other characterizes the Bible teacher who becomes a "prophet" when he deals with eschatology on subjects where the Bible is silent. During World War II, for example, a

---

[42] Unger, *Principles of Expository Preaching,* p. 155.

well-known Bible teacher wrote an article in a Christian periodical and identified Mussolini as the Antichrist just shortly before the dictator came to the end of his way. These "prophetic" utterances without Biblical foundation did not lead great numbers of his readers to have confidence in the writer or the message which he penned.

The God-called preacher who makes expository preaching the goal of his life will seek to cultivate discernment with regard to the silence of divine revelation. He will be careful to speak only when God speaks because of his confidence in the completeness of divine revelation. He will not be afraid to admit his own ignorance when the Bible is silent. A believer in verbal plenary inspiration, because of this conviction, will seek to understand and proclaim what the Bible teaches and only what it teaches.

One who emphasizes expository preaching in his ministry does not become a hobbyist. Some ministers have been guilty of emphasizing only their pet themes. However, when all the Bible is the preacher's text to be expounded during a given ministry in a church, there is no time or place for personal preference and theme. The preacher's personal preference will be all of the Bible as a lifetime theme.

4. Christ-centered in Content

One cannot be an expositor of the Bible without observing and proclaiming Christ as the Center of that Book. Christ, Himself, emphasizes this as He deals with the two disciples on the way to Emmaus. "Then he said unto them, O fools, and slow of heart to believe all that the prophets have spoken: Ought not Christ to have suffered these things, and to enter into his glory? And beginning at Moses and all the prophets, he expounded unto them in all the scriptures the things concerning himself" (Luke 24:25-28).

The rope used by the British Navy in years past was identified by a red strand twisted with the hundreds of others which made the rope. Someone has expressed this as an illustration of the Christ-centered unity of the Bible by saying it is a Book bound together with a scarlet cord. Another has said that no matter where you open the Bible, you will find it red with the blood of Christ. It is impossible for a preacher to practice expository preaching without touching many times on the redemptive work and the glorious Person of Christ. "Indeed, the most successful expositor will be the one who discerns most clearly that the grand subject of the Bible and its central unifying theme are the Person and work of Jesus Christ, the Redeemer; and that everywhere He is to be traced in type, symbol, promise and prophecy."[43] Let it be emphasized once again that this unity of the divine record and its revelation of Jesus Christ is a reality only because the divine record has been written under the superintendence of a single Author, the Holy Spirit of God.

One whose life's work is the preparation and delivery of sermons will find an inexhaustible supply, a doctrinal emphasis, a balanced message, and a unifying theme when he accepts verbal, plenary inspiration and recognizes its importance in his study of the Bible.

C. IT AFFECTS HIS PROCLAMATION BY GIVING HIM CONFIDENCE

A firm belief in verbal inspiration gives the preacher confidence and will encourage him to:

1. PROCLAIM THE WORD OF GOD CLEARLY.

The Bible simply states the great spiritual truths so necessary to the regeneration of the soul and the spiritual growth of the believer. The Bible preacher is challenged to preach God's truth in a clear, understandable fashion because it is God's message which must be communicated to those who need it.

---

[43] *Ibid.,* p. 201.

Because of a desire to seem profound a preacher may be tempted to make his pulpit pronouncements complicated and unrelated to life. In addressing the citizens at Caesar's burial, Mark Anthony said, "For I have neither wit nor words nor worth." If this were a Bible verse, in order to impress his audience a preacher might say, "For I have neither sagacity, nor verbosity, nor intrinsic value." This would probably prove that neither preacher nor hearer understood the message.

One is always impressed with the clarity with which Jesus taught his hearers. Take the Sermon on the Mount as an example (Matt. 5-7). How plainly and simply He stated the Beatitudes as He refers to "the poor in spirit . . . they that mourn . . . the meek . . . they which do hunger and thirst." These references deal with life and its problems. He was also a master with illustrations or visual aids. He used the common things to illustrate His messages, such as "salt . . . light . . . candle" (Matt. 5:13-15). He referred to the "jot" and "tittle" of the Hebrew alphabet (Matt. 5:18). In 6:19-30, He illustrated His message with "moth . . . rust . . . thieves . . . the fowls of the air . . . the lilies . . . the grass of the field." In 7:9 and 10, He mentioned "bread . . . stone . . . fish . . . serpent." In just a brief span of verses (7:13-18) He referred to "the gate . . . way . . . sheep . . . wolves . . . grapes . . . thorns . . . figs . . . thistles . . . tree . . . and fruit." To be sure, His recorded messages are brief, but they are clear and understandable.

If we believe the Bible to be the Word of God, then we will be challenged to proclaim it with confidence in a single, clear, understandable manner because we will want the hearer to obtain the message from God.

2. PROCLAIM THE WORD OF GOD FEARLESSLY.

Approximately two thousand times the Bible states, "Thus saith the Lord." This gives the Bible preacher authority which he cannot find in any other book or man-made religious system.

It is not likely that any of us will be called in this day to preach unto Nineveh, but wherever we preach, we may be assured of the same command as that given to Jonah. "Arise, go . . . and preach . . . the preaching that I bid thee" (Jonah 3:1). What greater authority could any man need or desire?

Jeremiah was frightened when he heard the call of God to preach to a sinful people. This is understandable when one observes their attitude toward God. God gave him reason to be courageous when He said, ". . . Thou shalt go to all that I shall send thee, and whatsoever I command thee thou shalt speak. Be not afraid of their faces; for I am with thee to deliver thee, saith the LORD" (Jer. 1:7-9; see also 1:17; 7:27, 28).

Jonah, Jeremiah and other prophets of the Bible, as well as Biblical preachers after them, have been able to speak fearlessly because of the command of God. Truth can always be proclaimed with authority, and adherence to the inspired Bible guarantees the truthfulness of the message. "This authority is not arrogant dogmatism, but rather humble confidence that one knows and proclaims the truth. One cannot honestly deal with the Scriptures without imbibing something of their authority."[44] Preaching with such an authority creates an audience. Men and women beset with problems and a host of uncertainties are looking for such a message. Unfortunately, too many find themselves in churches where the pastor is as troubled and as uncertain as his audience.

> Time was when men stood behind the sacred desk and opened God's Word and declared, "Thus saith the Lord," and men listened and were impressed and trembled; but men will not be impressed with a half-truth breathed out in uncertainty and with an apology. Men

---

[44] Faris D. Whitesell, *Art of Biblical Preaching* (Grand Rapids: Zondervan Publishing House, 1950), p. 29.

will not come to church to hear you philosophizing on your guesses and speculations.[45]

3. PROCLAIM THE WORD OF GOD EXPECTANTLY.

The Bible-believing preacher knows what God's Word will do because of its promise and performance. With Paul he has discovered that it is "the word of God, which effectually worketh also in you that believe" (1 Thess. 2:13; see further 1:5, 6). He knows it "is quick, and powerful, and sharper than any two-edged sword. . ." (Heb. 4:12). The Bible preacher is persuaded that the Lord "is strong that executeth his word. . ." (Joel 2:11). He appreciates the confidence given to the prophet of old when the Lord said, "Because ye speak this word, behold, I will make my words in thy mouth fire, and this people wood, and it shall devour them" (Jer. 5:14). He is aware that God's Word is powerful, for with the psalmist he can say, ". . . Thy word hath quickened me" (Psa. 119:50).

God has promised to use His Word (Isa. 55:11; Jer. 23:29). It is His tool; therefore, His servant can be confident. He can proclaim it with authority. "The true preacher has no fads to air; no fancies to unfold; no fallacies to express; but the facts of the gospel to proclaim."[46] As he prepares, prays and preaches, God's servant can await with confidence the performance of God's Word in doing God's work.

There are numerous examples of the work done by the power of His Word. In Acts 16 we have the record of three individual conversions showing the power of the Word as it was given by Paul and his companions. "Lydia . . . heard . . . whose heart the Lord opened. . ." (v. 14). "A certain damsel possessed with the spirit of divination . . .

---

[45] Charles F. Ball, "The Works of the Ministry," *Bibliotheca Sacra*, CVI, October-December, 1949 (Dallas: Dallas Theological Seminary), pp. 331, 332.

[46] F. E. Marsh, *One Thousand Bible Readings* (Grand Rapids: Zondervan Publishing House, 1953), p. 456.

Paul . . . said . . . I command thee in the name of Jesus Christ to come out of her. And he came out the same hour" (v. 16-18). "Believe on the Lord Jesus Christ, and thou shalt be saved . . . they spake unto him the word of the Lord. . ." (v. 31, 32). And every evidence is given that he believed. Lydia, an Asiatic; the damsel, a Greek of Philippi; and a Roman jailer, all experienced the power of God's Word. One was a business woman, another a slave, and the third a government employee, but the message was effective in each of their hearts. Lightfoot states that these miracles of the Word of God bring "the amelioration of women and the abolition of slavery." It would require volumes to recount the testimonies of those who have been transformed by the power of the Word of God since the apostolic period. The conversion of Augustine is an outstanding example in early church history. After living a wicked and licentious life, he was convicted by Christ in his thirty-third year. In the agony of uncertainty and unrest, he cried, "Thou, my Lord, how long yet? Oh, Lord, how long yet wilt thou be angry? Remember not the sins of my youth. How long, how long? Tomorrow, and again, tomorrow. Why not today? Why not now? Why not in this hour put an end to my shame?" He then read Romans 13:14, ". . . Put ye on the Lord Jesus Christ, and make not provision for the flesh, to fulfil the lusts thereof." The issue was settled and he became a Christian by trusting Christ as He is revealed in God's holy Word.

Charles Haddon Spurgeon had a remarkable conversion to Christ after living in a miserable experience of condemnation. This miracle of conversion took place when he was a boy of less than fifteen. A snowstorm made it impossible for him to go further in a journey. He stopped in a primitive Methodist chapel. A layman stood up to preach since the pastor could not reach the church because of the storm. The text was Isaiah 45:22, "Look unto me, and be ye saved, all the ends of the earth: for I am God, and there is none else." The preacher pointed to Spurgeon with the words, "Young man, you're in trouble. Look to Jesus Christ! Look! Look! Look!" Said Spurgeon, "Oh, I did 'Look'! I could almost have looked my eyes away! I felt like Pilgrim when the burden of guilt which he had borne so long was forever rolled from *my* shoulders."[47]

The Bible preacher may surely preach with confidence in the effectiveness of his message. "Biblical preaching is always an exciting adventure. It is fraught with infinite possibilities. The preacher can pour out his life and soul into it with a consciousness that God works with him and that only eternity will fully reveal the results."[48]

D. IT AFFECTS HIS APPLICATION BY GIVING HIM CONCERN

Altogether too many preachers in our time preach without urgency. They appear before only a Sunday morning audience, and that without concern for the future of their hearers. They go through the performance of the usual ritual without a passion for the souls of men, "Having a form of godliness, but denying the power thereof. . ." (2 Tim. 3:5). These weekly homilies leave the hearer little better off than he would be had he not heard them in the first place. Preachers who reject the Bible and substitute human ethics, sociological observations, and philosophical speculations are not men of Biblical persuasion and evangelistic compassion. What more can we expect from pulpits when the Bible is given only a religious nod in the lives of many churchgoers and briefly noticed on Sunday morning by the preachers?

---

[47] Richard Ellsworth Day, *Shadow of the Broad Brim,* (Philadelphia: The Judson Press, 1934), pp. 57, 58.

[48] Faris D. Whitesell, *Sixty-five Ways to Give an Evangelistic Invitation* (Grand Rapids: Zondervan Publishing House, 1915), p. 11.

Because of this conviction, the preacher who believes the Bible must appeal to his hearers to respond to the invitation to trust in the Christ of the Bible. He has:

1. A SCRIPTURAL EXAMPLE TO FOLLOW.

God gave the first appeal in Scripture expressing great concern for Adam when He asked, "Where art thou?" (Gen. 3:9). When Israel fell into sin in the worship of the golden calf, Moses appealed to the people to decide for God when he said, "Who is on the LORD's side? let him come unto me. . ." (Exod. 32:26). Joshua gave an appeal to his people when he said, "If it seem evil unto you to serve the LORD, choose you this day whom ye will serve. . ." (Josh. 24:15).

Jesus appealed to Peter and Andrew, "Follow me, and I will make you fishers of men" (Matt. 4:19). To Matthew He said, "Follow me" (Matt. 9:9), and he came and followed Him. To Zacchaeus He commanded, "Make haste, and come down; for today I must abide at thy house" (Luke 19:5). Jesus gave a parable with an illustration of the gospel invitation, "Go out into the highways and hedges, and compel them to come in, that my house may be filled" (Luke 14:23).

After giving a Biblical sermon, Peter expressed great concern in his appeal on the Day of Pentecost, "Save yourselves from this untoward generation" (Acts 2:40). In the synagogue at Ephesus Paul is found "disputing and persuading the things concerning the kingdom of God" (Acts 19:8). Agrippa felt the appeal of Paul's concern for he said, "Almost thou persuadest me to be a Christian" (Acts 26:28). Here is an example of an evangelistic appeal—an invitation from the greatest of expository preachers.

As though to emphasize the Bible as one great united appeal to the hearts of men, it closes with "And the Spirit and the bride say, Come. And let him that heareth say, Come. And let him that is athirst come. And whosoever will, let him take the water of life freely" (Rev. 22:17).

We believe that is ample Biblical reason for the preacher to give an invitation for men to publicly decide for Christ. "The preacher does not fully deliver the burden of his soul until he has given the invitation."[49] "The preacher should always be preaching for a verdict. He should expect decisions as a result of preaching the Word of God."[50]

2. A Personal Responsibility To Fulfill

Paul expressed the feeling of every God-called Bible preacher when he wrote, ". . . Necessity is laid upon me; yea, woe is unto me, if I preach not the gospel!" (1 Cor. 9:16). This passion is further expressed in his desire to preach the gospel in the regions beyond (2 Cor. 10:16). His ministry was constantly one of compassion. In his message to the Ephesians he reminded them, ". . . I kept back nothing that was profitable unto you, but have shewed you, and taught you publickly, and from house to house . . . I ceased not to warn every one night and day with tears" (Acts 20:20, 31).

Paul's great heart never seemed to lack an agony for souls. In his message to the Colossians he wrote, "Whereunto I also labour, *striving* according to his working, which worketh in me mightily. For I would that ye knew what great conflict I have for you, and for them at Laodicea. . ." (Col. 1:29; 2:1—italics ours). The word "strive" refers to conflict in an arena. It could mean running, wrestling, or boxing. Arthur Way translates it, "For this I am toiling. I am wrestling hard with all the soul-thrilling power which God in His might is enkindling me." Bishop Handley Moule calls Paul's agony "a sustained importunate courageous conflict; a strife with all and anything which would withstand his praying" for those he sought to win to Christ.

That his compassion to reach others was a lifelong experience is evident, for in his later years he expressed it

---

[49] *Ibid.*, p. 11.
[50] Homer A. Kent, Sr., *The Pastor and His Work* (Chicago: Moody Press, 1963), p. 119.

again to the Roman Christians when he wrote, "Whensoever I take my journey into Spain, I will come to you. . ." (Rom. 15:24). So far as we know, he never reached Spain; but his compassion had this in his personal missionary program. Paul had this conviction which enabled him to go through great suffering, face many enemies, meet the rebuff of those whom he loved because he believed he had a message from God and must communicate it to as many people as possible.

The Bible preacher has a similar responsibility to men in our time, but he has also a responsibility motivated by his own future appearance before the Lord, the terrible judgment of God upon the lost, the love of Christ revealed on the Cross, and the message of reconciliation which he as a Christian alone must give (2 Cor. 5:10, 11, 14). "The preacher should feel the burden of the tomorrows and the eternal destiny of those to whom he preaches."[51] His passion is not something produced by clever psychological tricks or revealed by a certain pitch or twang of a voice. It is not something worked up, pumped in, or pulled out of the man by a mere human emotion. "It comes out of the inner heart and soul of the speaker as he experiences the deepest reality of spiritual truth and is borne along by the Holy Spirit."[52] Keep in mind that this passion comes through truth and by the Holy Spirit. The Holy Spirit inspired the truth since He authored the Word of God. A preacher who keeps his heart in tune with Him, according to the Word, will be a preacher of concern and passion.

3. A Spiritual Need To Consider

What does a person who actually believes the Bible to be divinely inspired have to face with regard to the spiritual condition of lost men and women? The answer

---

[51] David M. Dawson, Jr., *More Power to the Preacher* (Grand Rapids: Zondervan Publishing House, 1956), p. 57.

[52] Whitesell, *Art of Biblical Preaching*, p. 109.

to this question will surely bring concern to every sincere Bible-believing preacher and should burden every member of his congregation as well.

This inspired record we profess to believe says that all men are lost (Luke 19:10); under condemnation (John 3:18); sinners who have come short of God's glory (Rom. 3:10, 23); aliens from God (Eph. 4:18); subjects of the judgment of God (Heb. 9:27); receiving the wages of sin (Rom. 6:23); and headed for the Lake of Fire (Rev. 20:15). Numerous other references can be cited to show the hopeless, helpless, and horrible condition of men without Christ. These references taken along with the many Scriptures which teach our responsibility to reach these men for Christ surely can do nothing less than give us unbearable concern in our preaching as well as our living.

William Booth began the Salvation Army in the east end of London. A small group of young people caught his vision to reach the outcast. Booth began a school to teach his followers to win the lost. One day while teaching them, he paused and dramatically said, "I wish I could send you all to Hell for two weeks." What a concern and compassion for souls such a trip would give them, and all of us, too, if we could take such a journey and get a vision of the lost estate of men!

How can we be other than concerned for the souls of men with these Biblical facts ringing in our ears? These truths must have gripped the soul of Richard Baxter of whom it was said, "He preached as a dying man to dying men, and as ne'er to preach again." These facts must have reached and touched the soul of John Knox when he said, "Give me Scotland, or I die!"

IV

THE IMPORTANCE OF INSPIRATION TO CHRISTIAN EXPERIENCE

The teaching of Scripture and the testimony of believers unite to say that the Bible has an important and irreplacable ministry in the life of the Christian. It is "Our test of the faith, our arm for the conflict, our mirror of the soul, our guide for the way and our strength for the life."[53] In order for the Bible to do all that it does for those who believe, it must be more than a book created by human genius. Only a verbally inspired revelation, a message from the omnipotent God, can produce the results which have been evident in the lives of Christians down through the centuries of time.

There are two Psalms (19, 119) which give rather detailed statements on Bibliology. They tell us what the Word of God is, what it does, and what it expects of those who accept it. For example, Psalm 19 defines God's Word as "the law . . . testimony . . . statutes . . . commandment . . .

---

[53] Guy King, *A Day At A Time* (London: Purnell & Sons, Ltd., 1956), October 25.

fear . . . judgments of the LORD." The power of God's Word in the life is seen from "conversion" to "reward."

Between these two experiences in the Christian life there are a number of other spiritual ministries which the Word of God performs for the believer. It instructs, for it makes wise the simple. It gives assurance by "rejoicing the heart." It provides discernment through "enlightening the eyes." It is the agent of sanctification since it is "clean, enduring for ever." Day by day satisfaction is given through the Word since it is "gold" and "honey." In view of the fact that the Psalm does not end with verse 6, it makes very clear that natural revelation described in the preceding verses though quite enough to remove man's excuses (Rom. 1:19, 20) it is not sufficient for the creation and sustenance of the spiritual life.

So far as the Christian life is concerned, there can be no spiritual beginning, growth, power or satisfaction without a personal trust in, and study of the Bible. There is no vital Christian experience apart from the Word of Truth. Jesus said, "If ye continue in my word, then are ye my disciples indeed" (John 8:31, 32). In this light several facts should be observed.

A. THE WORD OF GOD IS A SEED WHICH COMMUNICATES LIFE

"For you have been born again not of seed which is perishable, but imperishable, that is, through the living and abiding word of God" (1 Pet. 1:23, *New American Standard Bible*). "The seed is the word of God" (Luke 8:11).

The incorruptible seed stands out in contrast to the perishable grass and the flowers, beautiful though they are. The grass dries up and the flowers drop off, but the Word of the Lord lives on forever. The seed which is the Word of God is both living and life-giving. It abides eternally. "It is God's life which enters dead human souls through the

Word and makes them live. The life which is thus begotten is in them as infinite and eternal as God Himself."[54]

The Word of the living God communicates life to those who are dead in sins. Without it there can be no passing from death unto life. No imaginary experience, emotional reaction, or educational program can be a substitute for the receiving of the Word. It brings life and guarantees spiritual reality in the following manner:

1. It Convicts the Sinner.

On the day of Pentecost Peter preached the Word of God and concluded his sermon by saying, ". . . God hath made that same Jesus, whom ye have crucified, both Lord and Christ. Now when they heard this, they were pricked [stunned or cut] in their heart. . ." (Acts 2:36, 37). The word "prick" means to "pierce through, pierce with compunction and pain of heart." The Word of God is ". . . sharper than any twoedged sword, piercing even to the dividing asunder of soul and spirit" (Heb. 4:12). It is a sword which cuts and pierces even into the recesses of the human heart.

> The Word of God pierces through all that lies deepest in human nature, not actually separating soul from spirit and joints from marrow, but piercing and laying bare the inmost being, cutting through the most secret recesses of the spirit's life, penetrating the soul and, deeper still, the spirit, as through joints to their very marrow.[55]

It is the Word of God which so convinces men of sin that they confess their true spiritual condition. God spoke to Pharaoh in judgment and he cried, "I have sinned. . ." (Exod. 9:27; 10:16). Balaam made the same confession

---

[54] F. B. Meyer, *The First Epistle of Peter* (New York: Fleming H. Revell Company, 1912), p. 70.

[55] W. E. Vine, *The Epistle to the Hebrews* (Grand Rapids: Zondervan Publishing House, 1957), p. 44.

when the angel of the Lord spoke to him (Num. 22:34). Joshua spoke God's message to Achan and brought confession from his lips (Josh. 7:20). After Saul had disobeyed God, Samuel said, ". . . Thou hast rejected the word of the LORD. . ." and Saul replied, "I have sinned. . ." (1 Sam. 15:23, 24). The Lord sent Nathan to David and charged him with sin when he said, "Thou art the man." This word from God brought confession of sin from David in 2 Samuel 12:1, 7 and 13. If we want to return to Biblical conviction in our day we must return to Biblical preaching which produces it.

2. IT REVEALS THE SAVIOR.

John reminds us that the purpose of his gospel is that men "might believe that Jesus is the Christ, the Son of God. . ." (John 20:31). To the Jews of His day Jesus said, "Search the scriptures . . . they . . . testify of me" (John 5:39). They searched the Scriptures, for in so doing they thought eternal life would be granted as a result of their searching. Jesus reminds them, and us, that salvation is in Him and not in merit gained by Bible study. This is not a command of Jesus to study the Scriptures, though this we ought to do, but rather a statement of what His hearers were doing.

> These people and their successors have the *record* and yet miss the *revelation;* they have the garden without the flowers; the organ without the music; the body without the soul; the altar without the sacrifice. What is the good of that? What is the use of your going through the Bible if the Bible does not go through you?[56]

John the Baptist was a witness to Christ. The works which Christ performed were also an evidence of the Savior's deity. The Father's voice from Heaven spoke of Him. John

---

[56] W. Graham Scroggie, *St. John,* Introduction and Notes (New York: Harper and Row Publishers, 1931), p. 41.

has passed from the earth; the miracles which He performed while on earth are no longer being done; and the Father's voice is no longer heard. The last remaining witness to Christ is the Scriptures.

In commenting upon Timothy's spiritual heritage, Paul wrote, "And that from a child thou hast known the holy scriptures, which are able to make thee wise unto salvation through faith which is in Christ Jesus" (2 Tim. 3:15). The Word of God not only convicts of sin, but directs the sinner to trust the Savior. Since the whole Bible is the revelation of Christ, it is to be expected that men should be pointed to Him through all of the revelation whether they read the history and prophecy of the Old Testament or the gospels and epistles of the New Testament.

3. IT REGENERATES THE BELIEVER.

Jesus said, "It is the spirit that quickeneth . . . the words that I speak unto you, they are spirit, and they are life" (John 6:63). In these words Christ informs us that the Spirit, not the flesh, imparts spiritual life. Further, we are informed that the Holy Spirit uses the Word as the divine instrument to bring life to the soul. God begets "with the word of truth" (Jas. 1:18). Through God's "exceeding great and precious promises" we are made "partakers of the divine nature" (2 Pet. 1:4). Since the Word of God has such a vital place in the salvation of a soul, it must be preached with complete reliance on the ministry of the Holy Spirit to do this supernatural work of regeneration. "What is needed is less anecdotal preaching; less rhetorical embellishment, less reliance upon logic, and more direct, plain, pointed, *simple* declaration and exposition of the Word itself. Sinners will never be saved without this—'the flesh profiteth *nothing*'!"[57]

---

[57] Arthur Pink, *Exposition of the Gospel of John,* Vol. II (Swengel, Pennsylvania: Bible Truth Depot, 1923), pp. 89, 90.

The same truth is emphasized in the Old Testament also. In Psalm 119 there are a number of references to the quickening power of the Word of God. The words "quicken" or "quickened" are used at least eleven times in this Psalm. Most of the statements are direct references to God's Word as being the life-giving agent. "Quicken me according to thy word" is an oft-repeated petition of the Psalmist (vv. 25, 107, 149, 154, 156). He states what God has done for him when he says, "Thy word hath quickened me" (vv. 50, 93). In Ephesians 2:1, the lost sinner is declared to be "dead in trespasses and sins." The same chapter declares that by grace we are quickened or raised up together with Him. "Man is quickened out of his spiritual death and disunion into a spiritual life of union and communion with God."[58] God works effectually in those who believe. God is the power and His Word is the instrument which imparts spiritual life to those who are dead in sin.

4. It Assures the Reader.

God not only saves us through the instrumentality of His Word, but by that same means makes it possible for us to know that we are saved. "These things have I written to you that believe . . . that ye may know that ye have eternal life. . ." (1 John 5:13). Christ promised this assurance through His Word when He said, "He that heareth my word, and believeth on him that sent me, hath everlasting life, and shall not come into condemnation; but is passed from death unto life" (John 5:24). Hearing and believing the Word of God assures the Christian that he shall not be condemned, but is already the possessor of eternal life. This confidence increases as one reads the Bible, for "faith cometh by hearing" (Rom. 10:17).

The New Testament refers to "the full assurance of understanding" (Col. 2:2), "hope" (Heb. 6:11), and "faith"

---

[58] Emory H. Bancroft, *Elemental Theology,* Third Edition (Grand Rapids: Zondervan Publishing House, 1960), p. 196.

(Heb. 10:22); each of which must be based upon a solid and unchanging foundation. The Word of God gives spiritual understanding (Luke 24:44, 45), steadfast hope (Rom. 15:4), and enduring faith (Rom. 10:17). A Book which performs such supernatural works in the lives of those who believe must be much more than ordinary literature. It is, indeed, the divine seed which communicates divine life. Therefore, it is of great importance that we accept it as the inspired Word of God.

B. THE WORD OF GOD IS A LAVER WHICH CLEANSES DEFILEMENT

"Christ also loved the church, and gave himself for it; That he might sanctify and cleanse it with the washing of water by the word" (Eph. 5:25, 26). In the Old Testament tabernacle the laver made of the "looking glasses" of the women, and filled with water, was not only a means of removing defilement; but revealing it as well. The Word of God in the New Testament answers to the laver in both particulars (Eph. 5:26; Jas. 1:23, 24). As the Christian's laver, the Word of God:

1. PURGES THE BELIEVER FROM DEFILEMENT.

"Wherewithal shall a young man cleanse his way? by taking heed thereto according to thy word" (Psa. 119:9). "Now ye are clean through the word which I have spoken unto you" (John 15:3).

Before Jesus washed the disciples' feet, He had a special conversation with Simon Peter. At first Peter rejected the thought that Christ his Lord should wash his feet. Then Jesus said, "If I wash thee not, then thou hast no part with me" (John 13:8). Then Peter was willing to submit to the Savior's request, but as usual his impetuous nature went beyond what was required; for he wanted the Lord to wash his head, hands and feet. Jesus answered Peter's enthusiasm by saying, "He that is washed needeth not save to wash his feet. . ." (John 13:10). This incident in the ministry of Christ typifies the cleansing of daily defilement so needed by everyone of us today. That the Word is the Laver that cleanseth our defilement we see so clearly in Ephesians 5:26. This "washing" is not baptism since water used externally cannot produce internal and eternal life or wash away personal sin.

A Christian's holy walk is made possible because the Word of God enables him to walk in the light. As we walk in the light, the blood of Jesus Christ cleanseth us from sin (1 John 1:7).

> Whatever other means may be employed, and there are many, they must be viewed as subordinate to the action of the "truth," or as making room for its purging process. Thus when affliction as a part of the process is brought into view, it is only as a means to the end of the soul's subjection and obedience to the Word.[59]

It is not only the agent used by the Holy Spirit to save the soul of the believing sinner from judgment, but it is the means used of God to save the soul of the saint from damage as he reads and obeys it. "So strip yourselves of everything impure and all the evils prevailing around you, and in humble spirit welcome the message which when rooted in your hearts is able to save your souls. Keep on obeying this message; do not merely listen to it, and so deceive yourselves" (Jas. 1:21, 22—*Charles B. Williams Translation*). Surrounded as we are with sin, we should see the importance of the inspired Word of God as the divine medium for daily cleansing.

2. PRESERVES THE BELIEVER FROM SIN.

"Thy word have I hid in mine heart, that I might not sin against thee. . . Order my steps in thy word: and let not any iniquity have dominion over me" (Psa. 119: 11, 133).

---

[59] Pink, *The Exposition of the Gospel of John,* Volume III, p. 339.

"For the commandment is a lamp; and the law is light. . . To keep thee from the evil. . ." (Prov. 6:23, 24).

The laver in the Tabernacle stood between the people in the camp and the articles of furniture which speak of fellowship with God. "Thou shalt . . . put it [the laver] between the tabernacle of the congregation and the altar, and thou shalt put water therein" (Exod. 30:18). It stood as a barrier to the priest entering the place of worship unclean. As the pure cleansing agent from the Lord it has inducements to holiness keeping us from sin by its promises to overcome temptation; its pronouncements of divine consequences because of disobedience; and its predictions of reward in the future for loyalty to its teaching now. Many of us have been arrested as we were following a wrong direction in our life by the Spirit of God Who brought a particular Scripture to our attention. For example, some have stopped short as they considered ". . . whatsoever a man soweth, that shall he also reap" (Gal. 6:7). Multitudes of God's people have not been "weary in well doing" because they claimed the promise that "in due season we shall reap, if we faint not" (Gal. 6:9).

3. PROTECTS THE BELIEVER FROM ERROR.

"Sanctify them through thy truth: thy word is truth" (John 17:17). Paul admonished the Ephesian Christians to watch for wolves who would enter in and to be careful of perverse teachers rising out of their own ranks who would not spare the flock but would draw away disciples after them (Acts 20:29, 30). How did he prepare to remedy this infiltration of error? He said to them, "I commend you to God, and to the word of his grace, which is able to build you up. . ." (Acts 20:32). Those who are "built up" in their knowledge of God through His Word will be able to detect and reject error. Christians with scanty knowledge of the Word of God are easy targets for the darts of false teachers.

The exhortations to "Study . . . rightly dividing the word of truth," and "Preach the word" (2 Tim. 2:15; 4:2) are given in the context of warnings against apostasy (2 Tim. 3:1-9). The Word of God is the only guaranteed protection against religious error. No one of us is strong enough intellectually or spiritually to defend the faith without implicit confidence in this Book. As the Laver it keeps our spiritual lives clean so that the seed of false teaching will have no fertile ground in which to sprout. "To have the Word of life in our minds is good; to have the life of the Word in our hearts is better; but to have the life of the Word in living characters in the life is best."[60] It is also the Sword of the Spirit which God expects us to use in our warfare against the enemy (Eph. 6:17). So the laver of the Word keeps us that we may do battle against the enemy of the soul. Nothing short of a Spirit-inspired revelation could be this effective against every attack upon the believer in Christ.

C. THE WORD OF GOD IS A LAMP WHICH GIVES ILLUMINATION

The Word of God is said to be a lamp and a light (Psa. 119:105). It is a "light" which gives general illumination for the whole pathway of life, and a "lamp" or "candle" which gives particular guidance for one step at a time. In another reference we are told that "the commandment of the Lord is pure, enlightening the eyes" (Psa. 19:8).

The Word of God definitely teaches us that there are certain things which we are to do. For example, we read, ". . . Men ought always to pray, and not to faint" (Luke 18:1). There are prohibitions also clearly stated in the Scriptures. "Be ye not unequally yoked together with unbelievers" (2 Cor. 6:14). These statements are classified under the revealed will of God. We must also consider

---

[60] F. E. Marsh, *Pearls, Points and Parables* (Grand Rapids: Baker Book House, 1954), p. 263.

what is now the concealed will of God. By this we mean there are directions which God will make known to us in the future, but He has not recorded particular admonitions in His Word concerning them. These are discovered through prayer and by careful study of the Word of God. This was Paul's concern for the Ephesian believers when he wrote, "Wherefore be ye not unwise, but understanding what the will of the Lord is" (Eph. 5:17). The precepts of the Word of God are clearly stated, but our daily lives must be lived within the principles of this wonderful revelation. For a Christian to know the will of God in his life there must be:

1. DESIRE FOR THE WORD OF GOD.

"As newborn babes, desire [crave, long for] the sincere milk of the word. . ." (1 Pet. 2:2). The Word of God is to be more desired than gold (Psa. 19:10; 119:72). In order to have the desires of our hearts we must "delight in the Lord" (Psa. 37:4). To delight in the Lord we must desire His Word for we cannot know Him apart from it. It is impossible for any Christian to positively know the will of God if he does not have a desire or craving for God's Word. Since God speaks to His people through the Scriptures, how can we expect to be informed of His plan for us if we neglect His means of communication? The precepts and principles revealed in the Bible must be desired if the pathway of the believer is to be plain. If we want the Word and the will of God as much as we may crave gold, there is little question as to whether or not we will find it. He will certainly show us.

"What the food is to the infant, the Word of God is to the spiritual nature."[61] Infants eventually have much more than a milk diet. However, the Christian never outgrows his need for the unadulterated milk of the Word. Until we see Him face to face we will need our daily por-

---

[61] F. E. Marsh, *The Spiritual Life* (Des Moines: Boone Publishing Company, 1958), p. 219.

tion. Someone has said, "The world is but the nursery in which the heirs of God are spending their first lisping years of their existence." Since we are always pressing on toward the goal of perfection we shall always need the Word of God as the divinely appointed means of reaching it. The first step, therefore, in knowing God's will for today is to desire God's Word for our spiritual growth.

2. A Time for Meditation in the Word of God.

As Joshua faced the unknown in the land of Canaan and needed direction each step of the way, the Lord said, "This book of the law shall not depart out of thy mouth; but thou shalt meditate therein day and night. . ." (Josh. 1:8). Again we are informed that the "blessed" man is one whose walk is right before God and man. He is so because he meditates in the Word of God day and night (Psa. 1:1, 2; cf. Psa. 119:15, 78, 148). We may be able to boast of the negative and not walk in the way of the ungodly, but we must also experience the positive and have the life characterized by meditation in God's Word if we are to know His will. Thomas A. Kempis stated it, "I have no rest but in a nook with the Book." An old Puritan writer said,

> Meditation helps judgment, wisdom and faith to ponder, discern and credit the things which reading and hearing supply and furnish. It assists the memory to look by the jewels of divine truth in our own treasury. It has a dazzling power, turns special truth into nourishment; and lastly, helps the renewed heart to grow upward and increase its power to know the things which are freely given to us of God.[62]

When we are saturated with God's Word and make it a part of our daily life, it is available to us at a moment's notice when we need to know God's will and make a decision. Meditation makes the Word of God so much a part

---

[62] Charles Haddon Spurgeon, *The Treasury of David*, Vol. I (New York: Funk and Wagnalls, 1892), p. 7.

of a Christian that he will not make decisions without its voice being heard. Thus, the art of meditation is important to the knowledge of God's will.

3. OBEDIENCE TO THE WORD OF GOD.

"Blessed are they that hear the word of God, and keep it" (Luke 11:28). "If ye know these things, happy are ye if ye do them" (John 13:17). These statements declare that true joy in the Christian life is dependent upon obedience to the Word of God. Obedience to what we now know is essential to obtain understanding of what we do not presently know. Christ made this clear in John 7:17. "If any man will do his will, he shall know of the doctrine. . . ." Here Jesus states that "The fundamental condition for obtaining spiritual knowledge is a genuine heart desire to carry out the revealed will of God in our lives."[63]

God will never reveal His will to the one who desires to know it if his reason for knowing it is to decide whether or not he wants to do it. We must be willing to do it before He will reveal it. "He leads the humble in what is right, and the humble He teaches His way" (Psa. 25:29—*Amplified Version*). A humble Christian is one who is submissive to God and His will. "Meek spirits are in high favor with the Father of the meek and lowly Jesus, for He sees in them the image of His only begotten Son. They know their need of guidance, then are willing to submit their own understandings to the divine will, and therefore the Lord condescends to be their guide."[64]

Proverbs 3:5 and 6 summarizes these truths which are so important to the child of God in his search for daily direction. If our ways are to be directed, there must be *dependence* upon God for we are commanded to "Trust in the LORD" (Prov. 3:5), and this trust comes by the Word of God (Rom. 10:17). No one will ever know God's will

---

[63] Pink, *op. cit.*, Vol. II, p. 121.
[64] Spurgeon, *op. cit.*, Vol. I, p. 444.

without *dedication,* "with all thine heart," (Prov. 3:5) where the Word of God is hidden (Psa. 119:11). He who would know God's plan for his life must *doubt* his own wisdom, "lean not unto . . . [his] own understanding," (Prov. 3:5) and pray, ". . . Give me understanding according to thy word" (Psa. 119:169). God gives *discernment* to those who in all their ways "acknowledge [recognize] him," (Prov. 3:6) for the Word of God is a "discerner [judge] of the thoughts and intents of the heart" (Heb. 4:12). Then, and only then, He will *direct* or rightly divide the paths we face in our pilgrim journey, showing which one we should take.

Obedience is the only alternative open to the submissive Christian. It is one of the consequences of being regenerated: a proof of the reality of salvation. "Quicken me after thy lovingkindness; so shall I keep the testimony of thy mouth" (Psa. 119:88). We must obey for "The Bible is the inerrant, infallible Word of God, the perfect revelation of the divine heart and mind of God, and of His great will for His children throughout the earth."[65] The inspiration and authority of the Scriptures demands obedience to its teaching on the part of a Christian. This is the secret of being guided into God's will. Where there is disobedience, there is no direction.

D. THE WORD OF GOD IS A DIET WHICH IMPARTS STRENGTH

The sustaining power of the Word of God is seen in the relationship of two Old Testament texts. "Thy words were found, and I did eat them; and thy word was unto me the joy and rejoicing of mine heart . . . The joy of the LORD is your strength" (Jer. 15:16; Neh. 8:10). As the human body needs food for physical strength so does the spiritual life of a Christian need spiritual food to be sustained in an unfriendly world. That the Word of God is that necessary

---

[65] G. Christian Weiss, *The Perfect Will of God* (Chicago: Moody Press, 1950), p. 75.

food is quite evident since it is called bread (Matt. 4:4);
meat (1 Cor. 3:2); milk (1 Pet. 2:2); water (Eph. 5:26);
and honey (Psa. 19:10). What a diet it is for spiritual
strength in the daily encounter with the problems of life!
Our trials are not unlike those in Biblical times. "The
divine life within us needs to be ministered unto and sustained just as much as the natural life, and the food for
the believer in Christ is nothing more and nothing less
than the Word of God which is milk to nourish, food to
strengthen, and meat to build up."[66] Men and women in
every age have faced times of trial, but their trust in the
Christ revealed in the Bible has provided a remedy for such
matters as the following.

1. DISCOURAGEMENT

At least two disciples left Jerusalem after the crucifixion,
depressed because they thought it was "all over." Christ had
died and they did not know He was resurrected. They were
walking toward Emmaus talking about their hopelessness,
and were sad about their plight (Luke 24:17). Discouragement always gets worse when we walk away from the Cross
and the empty tomb. It is always magnified, too, when we
share our discouragement with someone else.

The remedy for discouragement then and now is the
presence and message of Jesus Christ. After they heard an
exposition by the greatest of all preachers, they exclaimed,
"Did not our heart burn within us, while he talked with us
by the way, and while he opened to us the scriptures?" (Luke
24:32). Similarly, He appeared to the disciples in Jerusalem
and said, "Peace be unto you. And when he had so said, he
shewed unto them his hands and his side" (John 20:19, 20).
Here we observe that it is His Word and His Work which
brought peace to troubled disciples living in a world which
drove them to the Upper Room. The secret of peace is un-

---

[66] Henderson, *op. cit.,* p. 200.

changed. It is still hearing and believing His Word about His work which He has done for, in, and through His people.

2. Discipline

Testing is as much a part of the Christian life as the blessing which He bestows. In fact, the blessings are often greater because of the testings. Observe how this is emphasized in Psalm 119. Through testing, the Word of God brings consolation, for "This is my comfort in my affliction: for thy word hath quickened me" (v. 50). Trials bring us back to obeying the Word when we have strayed aside. "Before I was afflicted I went astray: but now have I kept thy word" (v. 67). Afflictions help us to learn more about God's Word. "It is good for me that I have been afflicted; that I might learn thy statutes" (v. 71). Discipline reveals the faithfulness of God as taught in the Word of God for His "judgments are right, and . . . thou in faithfulness hath afflicted me" (v. 75). No testing is too great for God to handle; for one declared, "I am afflicted very much: quicken me, O Lord, according unto thy word" (v. 107).

Every Scripture is profitable for . . . "instruction" (2 Tim. 3:16). The Greek word used here for *instruction* is translated "chastening." "If ye endure chastening, God dealeth with you as with sons. . ." (Heb. 12:7). It is a word which refers to the training up, education, and nurture of children (Eph. 6:4). The Word of God is the instrument used by the Holy Spirit to nurture the children of God. Without it there is no spiritual maturity. As we feed upon the manna from Heaven we are able to endure the discipline which it provides, and thus we grow in grace and in the knowledge of Christ.

3. Distress

Although the Christian's citizenship is in Heaven he still lives on earth. He is often faced with the same distresses as men and women of the world. Paul did not say that "ye sorrow not." He did say, ". . . Ye sorrow not, even as others which have no hope" (1 Thess. 4:13). We sorrow, but not hopelessly. In comforting sorrowing saints in New Testament times, Paul directed them to the Word of God. "For this we say unto you by the word of the Lord . . . Wherefore comfort one another with these words" (1 Thess. 4:15, 18). In the distress of separation by death, men today do not find comfort in human literature or empty sayings. They find it in the Word of the living God. "What time I am afraid, I will trust in thee. In God I will praise his word, in God I have put my trust; I will not fear what flesh can do unto me" (Psa. 56:3, 4).

These are days of fear. Some fear the nighttime only to awaken to greater fear in the day. Sickness, death, war, poverty, the loss of friends, are only a few of the themes which haunt the trials of the unbeliever. The Christian should not find it so. He says, ". . . Though I walk through the valley of the shadow of death, I will fear no evil . . ." (Psa. 23:4). We can put our trust in God only as we know Him through the Word. "Thy words were found, and I did eat them; and thy word was unto me the joy and rejoicing of mine heart" (Jer. 15:16). Fears will not be conquered, and sorrow will not flee away just because we possess a Bible. We must devour it through study and meditation.

Let us also remind ourselves that God comforts us, not that we might be comfortable, but comforters (2 Cor. 1:4). The Word of God does us more good when we devour it, and then declare it. Simply to know it gives us spiritual indigestion. F. E. Marsh succinctly stated it, "Let us ponder the Word of God prayerfully, live it out carefully, practice it thoroughly, study it minutely, abide in it constantly, long for it ardently, use it manfully, believe it wholly, and mind it obediently; and then the life will be aglow with love, and labor for Christ will be a lightsome task."[67]

---

[67] Marsh, *The Spiritual Life,* p. 219.

A study of the importance of inspiration in the Christian life reveals that the Word of God is far more than a series of beautiful thoughts, a fine spiritual influence, or a Book of outdated religious ideas. In order for the Word of God to do what it has done, and is doing in the lives of men and women, it must be of a supernatural origin and a revelatory communication breathed out by God Himself. Lives will not be transformed by mere words. Believers cannot be maintained in their spiritual convictions by a Book without authority. Sinners cannot be convicted of their lost condition by mythology. An anonymous poem, "God's Wonderful Word" declares what the Word of God means to a sincere believer in Jesus Christ.

When I am tired the Bible is my bed;
Or in the dark the Bible is my light;
When I am hungry it is vital bread;
Or fearful, it is armor for the fight.
When I am sick 'tis healing medicine;
Or lonely, thronging friends I find therein.
If I would work the Bible is my tool;
Or play, it is a harp of happy sound.

If I am ignorant it is my school,
If I am sinking it is solid ground.
If I am cold the Bible is my fire;
And it is wings if boldly I aspire.
Should I be lost the Bible is my guide;
Or naked it is raiment rich and warm.
Am I imprisoned, it is ranges wide;
Or tempest-tossed, a shelter from the storm.

Would I adventure, 'tis a gallant sea;
Or would I rest, it is a flowery lea.
Does gloom oppress? The Bible is a sun,

Or ugliness? It is a garden fair.
Am I athirst? How cool its currents run!
Or stifled? What a vivifying air!
Since thus thou givest of thyself to me,
How should I give myself
Great Book, to thee!

ANONYMOUS

BIBLIOGRAPHY

Ball, Charles F. "The Works of the Ministry," *Bibliotheca Sacra*, Volume CVI. Dallas: Dallas Theological Seminary, October-December, 1949.

Bancroft, Emory H. *Christian Theology*. Revised edition. Grand Rapids: Zondervan Publishing House, 1961.

————. *Elemental Theology*. Third edition. Grand Rapids: Zondervan Publishing House, 1960.

Collett, Sidney. *All About the Bible*. Twentieth edition. New York: Fleming H. Revell Company [n.d.].

Dawson, David M., Jr. *More Power to the Preacher*. Grand Rapids: Zondervan Publishing House, 1956.

Day, Gwynn McLendon. *The Wonder of the Word*. New York: Fleming H. Revell Company, 1907.

Day, Richard Ellsworth. *Shadow of the Broad Brim*. Philadelphia: The Judson Press, 1934.

Fairbairn, Patrick. *The Pastoral Epistles*. Edinburgh: T. & T. Clark, 1874.

Fitch, William. *The Impregnable Rock of Holy Scripture*. Toronto: Toronto Bible College, 1965.

Gaussen, Louis. *The Inspiration of the Holy Scriptures*. Chicago: Moody Press, 1949.

Harrison, Everett F. "The Phenomena of Scripture," *The Revelation and the Bible*. Edited by Carl F. H. Henry. Grand Rapids: Baker Book House, 1958.

Henderson, George. *The Wonderful Word.* Covington, Kentucky: Calvary Book Room [n.d.].

Kent, Homer A., Sr. *The Pastor and His Work.* Chicago: Moody Press, 1963.

King, Guy. *A Day At A Time.* London: Purnell & Sons, Ltd., 1956.

Marsh, F. E. *One Thousand Bible Readings.* Grand Rapids: Zondervan Publishing House, 1953.

————. *Pearls, Points and Parables.* Grand Rapids: Baker Book House, 1954.

————. *The Spiritual Life.* Des Moines: Boone Publishing Company, 1958.

Meyer, F. B. *Expository Preaching.* London: Hodder and Stoughton [n.d.].

————. *The First Epistle of Peter.* New York: Fleming D. Revell Company, 1912.

Orr, James. *The Progress of Dogma.* New York: George H. Doran Company, 1901.

Packer, J. I. *Fundamentalism and the Word of God.* Grand Rapids: William B. Eerdmans Publishing House, 1958.

Pardington, George P. *Outline Studies in Christian Doctrine.* Harrisburg: Christian Publications, 1926.

Pierson, A. T. *The Bible and Spiritual Criticism.* London: James Nisbet & Company, 1906.

————. *Knowing the Scriptures.* New York: Gospel Publishing House, 1910.

————. *The Inspired Word.* South Nyack: Christian Alliance Publishing Company [n.d.].

Pink, Arthur. *Exposition of the Gospel of John.* Volumes II and III. Swengel, Pennsylvania: Bible Truth Depot, 1923.

Ryrie, Charles C. "The Importance of Inerrancy," *Bibliotheca Sacra,* Volume CXX. Dallas: Dallas Theological Seminary, April-June, 1963.

————. *Neo-Orthodoxy, What It Is, and What It Does.* Chicago: Moody Press, 1956.

Scroggie, W. Graham. *St. John.* Introduction and Notes. New York: Harper and Row Publishers, 1931.

Spurgeon, Charles Haddon. *The Treasury of David.* Volume I. New York: Funk and Wagnalls, 1892.

Strauss, Lehman. *God's Plan For The Future.* Grand Rapids: Zondervan Publishing House, 1965.

Strong, Augustus Hopkins. *Systematic Theology.* Philadelphia: Griffith and Rowland Press. 1907.

Unger, Merrill F. "The Inspiration of the Old Testament," *Bibliotheca Sacra,* Volume CVII. Dallas: Dallas Theological Seminary, October-December, 1950.

————. *Principles of Expository Preaching.* Grand Rapids: Zondervan Publishing House, 1955.

Urquhart, John. *The Wonders of Prophecy.* Fifth edition. New York: Christian Publishing Company [n.d.].

Vincent, Marvin R. *Word Studies in the New Testament.* Volume IV. New York: Charles Scribner's Sons, 1905.

Vine, W. E. *The Epistle to the Hebrews.* Grand Rapids: Zondervan Publishing House, 1957.

Warfield, B. B. *The Inspiration and Authority of the Bible.* Philadelphia: The Presbyterian and Reformed Publishing House, 1948.

Weiss, G. Christian. *The Perfect Will of God.* Chicago: Moody Press, 1950.

Whitesell, Faris D. *Art of Biblical Preaching.* Grand Rapids: Zondervan Publishing House, 1950.

————. *Sixty-Five Ways to Give An Evangelistic Invitation.* Grand Rapids: Zondervan Publishing House, 1915.

Witmer, John A. "The Twentieth Century—Battleground of Bibliography," *Bibliotheca Sacra,* Volume CXI. Dallas: Dallas Theological Seminary, April-June, 1954.

Young, Edward J. *Thy Word is Truth.* Grand Rapids: William B. Eerdmans Publishing House, 1957.